Engaging Diverse Learners

Engaging Diverse Learners

Enhanced Approaches to Classroom Management

*Edited by Joanna Alcruz
and Maggie Blair*

ROWMAN & LITTLEFIELD
Lanham • Boulder • New York • London

Published by Rowman & Littlefield
An imprint of The Rowman & Littlefield Publishing Group, Inc.
4501 Forbes Boulevard, Suite 200, Lanham, Maryland 20706
www.rowman.com

86-90 Paul Street, London EC2A 4NE

Copyright © 2022 by Joanna Alcruz and Maggie Blair

All rights reserved. No part of this book may be reproduced in any form or by any electronic or mechanical means, including information storage and retrieval systems, without written permission from the publisher, except by a reviewer who may quote passages in a review.

British Library Cataloguing in Publication Information Available

Library of Congress Cataloging-in-Publication Data

Names: Alcruz, Joanna, editor. | Blair, Maggie, editor.
Title: Engaging diverse learners : enhanced approaches to classroom management / edited by Joanna Alcruz and Maggie Blair.
Description: Lanham, Maryland : Rowman & Littlefield, 2022. | Includes bibliographical references and index. | Summary: "Engaging Diverse Learners presents innovative approaches to classroom management by changing the classroom paradigm from a teacher-centered "managed"
    environment to a student-centered "empowering" classroom"-- Provided by publisher.
Identifiers: LCCN 2022019205 (print) | LCCN 2022019206 (ebook) | ISBN 9781475847673 (cloth) | ISBN 9781475847680 (paperback) | ISBN 9781475847734 (ebook)
Subjects: LCSH: Classroom management. | Student-centered learning. | Teacher-student relationships. | Motivation in education. | Culturally relevant pedagogy.
Classification: LCC LB3013 .E538 2022 (print) | LCC LB3013 (ebook) | DDC 371.102/4--dc23/eng/20220609 LC record available at https://lccn.loc.gov/2022019205 LC ebook record available at https://lccn.loc.gov/2022019206

*To Joseph, Janek, Julianka, and Karolinka, who
keep me anchored in what matters most.
—Joanna*

*To my daughter, Alexandra Elizabeth, who took me on a long, unplanned
professional journey. I am grateful to have had her in my life.
—Maggie*

Contents

List of Tables	ix
List of Figures	xi
Foreword *Andrea Honigsfeld*	xiii
Acknowledgments	xvii
Introduction *Joanna Alcruz and Maggie Blair*	1
Motivating Students for Classroom Engagement *Joanna Alcruz and Mubina Schroeder*	7
Fostering Relationships, Engagement, and Community to Enhance Classroom Management *Eve Dieringer, Michael Ferretti, and Kathleen Neagle Sokolowski*	29
Personalizing Learning for Classroom Management: An Evolution *Maggie Blair and Kevin Sheehan*	55
Classroom Management for Culturally and Linguistically Diverse Learners *Carrie L. McDermott Goldman and Lisa A. Peluso*	79

Communication Strategies Supporting Students for Grade-Level Transitions *Youn-Joo Park*	93
Fostering Social-Emotional Learning (SEL) for Classroom Management *Amandia Speakes-Lewis, Amy Meyers, and Carrie Sollin*	115
Index	139
About the Contributors	147

List of Tables

Table 2.1. Strategies to promote motivation.

Table 3.1. Types of Restorative Circles.

Table 4.1. Universal design for learning: An effective planning tool.

Table 4.2. Co-teaching models supporting specifically designed instruction.

Table 5.1. Self-reflection and suggestions for practice in culturally and linguistically diverse classrooms.

Table 5.2. The components and elements of the culturally responsive Sustaining framework.

Table 7.1. Emotional signs.

Table 7.2. Behavioral indicators.

Table 7.3. Compassion scenarios.

Table 7.4. Mission statements.

Table 7.5. What teachers can do to encourage a safe environment.

Table 7.6. Examples of being culturally responsive.

Table 7.7. Social-emotional learning skills.

List of Figures

Figure 2.1. Self-determination theory dimensions.

Figure 2.2. Motivational theories related to expectancy.

Figure 2.3. 2 × 2 achievement goal model.

Figure 2.4. Self-regulated learning model.

Figure 3.1. Family journal entry from the Alcruz family.

Figure 3.2. The social discipline window.

Figure 3.3. Fishbowl Circle.

Figure 3.4. Sequential Restorative Circle.

Figure 4.1. Understanding by design: Backward design.

Figure 4.2. The learning cycle.

Figure 5.1. Race and ethnicity change in the United States from 2000 to 2017.

Figure 5.2. English-language learner populations by state, 2000.

Figure 5.3. English-language learner populations by state, 2016.

Figure 6.1. Resource commitment level of communication strategies.

Figure 6.2. Communication praxis in K–12 versus college.

Figure 7.1. School and community collaboration for promoting social-emotional learning (SEL).

Foreword

Andrea Honigsfeld

> Education is the passport to the future, for tomorrow belongs to those who prepare for it today.
>
> —Malcolm X

I am honored to be invited by coeditors Joanna Alcruz and Maggie Blair to write the foreword to their two-part series on classroom management for diverse learners. It was personally and professionally affirming to do so, since close to a decade ago, I coedited a similar volume with Audrey Cohan (Cohan & Honigsfeld, 2012), also published by Rowman and Littlefield, titled *Breaking the Mold of Education: Innovative and Successful Practices for Student Engagement, Empowerment, and Motivation for the 21st Century*.

My excitement and curiosity kept growing with each new chapter I was reading—more and more eager to learn what might have remained unchanged in our response to students' needs, what has evolved, and what else must be done to further support learners, so they all may have a successful, enriching learning experience in their K–12 years.

Recently, I have been researching the many challenges that stakeholders—students, teachers, administrators, school-based support personnel, families, and community members—face in education. Or a better way to phrase the question for the purpose of this foreword could be this: What continues to be one of the greatest challenges in the field of education today? You might be considering a variety of factors, ranging from teacher shortages to inequities and poverty, from increasing workloads to stress, or from moving from in-person instruction to blended learning with successful technology integration. There is certainly no shortage of challenges, especially under current COVID-19 conditions.

It is well documented that many new and even experienced teachers are leaving the profession at an alarming rate. While there may be complex and complicated reasons for their decisions, it might not be surprising that one of the most frequently reported causes for quitting is challenges teachers face with classroom management (Sciuchetti & Yssel, 2019).

Reading the chapters of this book made me ponder these questions:

- What if we could do a better job of preparing future teachers, so they could build strong, vibrant learning communities in their classrooms that honor student diversity?
- What if we could improve the way we support new educators, so they could better respond to the academic, cultural, linguistic, and emotional complexities of today's classrooms?

Classroom management is frequently mistaken for managing behaviors, preventing disruption, or disciplining students who misbehave or otherwise break some well-established rules. This narrow definition is not outdated and limited to maintaining order, when in fact it may be best approached through everything else that is happening in the classroom and the school.

And by *everything*, I mean attending to the environment, experiences, engagement, equity, empowerment, and many more aspects of our day-to-day practice in the classroom, in the school, and in our larger educational communities (coincidentally, many of which seem to begin with the letter E). The question is this: How do we accomplish everything consistently, compassionately, and in a culturally responsive and sustaining manner? The editors and chapter contributors of this volume well understand the problem and masterfully combine their expertise to share research-informed, evidence-based answers that connect theory and practice.

The chapters are compelling and complete with richly illustrated examples. This book will help educators who are just starting out or perhaps returning to the field to accomplish the following:

1. Create and maintain a supportive, fair school and classroom culture that is conducive to learning for all.
2. Cultivate, not control, the learning environment where relationships come first.
3. Appreciate collaboration with colleagues and instill the value of collaboration in their students as well.
4. Serve students in an equitable way of recognizing a range of unique needs as well as the talents and passions of all students.
5. Engage students in exciting and enriching learning experiences that expand their minds and hearts.

6. Empower teachers to motivate their students, who, in turn, become empowered to take charge of their own learning journeys.

I enthusiastically invite you to join me in exploring the forthcoming pages of this inspiring volume. The chapters will keep you engaged in critically reflecting on what works and how to implement successful approaches to classroom management.

REFERENCES

Cohan, A., & Honigsfeld, A. (2012). *Breaking the mold of education: Innovative and successful practices for student engagement, empowerment, and motivation for the 21st century.* Rowman and Littlefield.

Sciuchetti, M. B., & Yssel, N. (2019). The development of preservice teachers' self-efficacy for classroom and behavior management across multiple field experiences. *Australian Journal of Teacher Education, 44*(6), 19–34. http://dx.doi.org/10.14221/ajte.2018v44n6.2

Acknowledgments

Joanna

I first and foremost thank my husband Joseph for his endless support in all my academic endeavors. I thank my children Janek, Julianka, and Karolinka, who peeked over my shoulder multiple times during this project and motivated me to continue. My sincere appreciation goes also to my coeditor, Maggie Blair, who, in the midst of the COVID-19 pandemic, kept us focused with her boundless energy and humor. I thank all my colleagues who contributed to this volume for sharing their knowledge and expertise, which came from the heart of loving what they do best—uplifting others through teaching.

Maggie

I begin my acknowledgments with my life partner of almost fifty years, my husband, Tommy, without whom my life would never have been the same. I am grateful to my own boys, T and Timmy, and their special life partners, Tasha and Nathalie, who have given me Lachlan, Sawyer, and Camille, my beautiful grandchildren, who continue to teach me to look at the world through fresh eyes. Thank you to my very special coeditor, Dr. Joanna Alcruz, whose calm and focused approach to this project brought it to fruition. And finally, to all those I have met, worked with, and learned from over the years, thank you all! I am most grateful to have had each and every one of you in my life!

Introduction

Joanna Alcruz and Maggie Blair

It is with great delight that we share this manuscript with you. This *Engaging Diverse Learners: Enhanced Approaches to Classroom Management* book, along with the *Student-Centered Classrooms: Research-Driven and Inclusive Strategies for Classroom Management* book (Alcruz & Blair, 2022), came about in March 2018 after Molloy University School of Education and Human Services responded to the needs of their preservice and newly minted in-service educators who expressed the need for learning more about classroom management. Soon, a one-day conference on "Conscious and Responsive Classrooms" was presented at Molloy, where many educators, researchers, and experts in the field came together to discuss what it means to strategically organize classrooms and respond to student needs.

Soon after the conference, we received an invitation from Rowman & Littlefield to update a classroom management book. We realized that the manuscript we received to work on was heavily outdated and no longer reflective of changes in the field of education and classroom management. This is when we decided to tap the expertise of our colleagues. We invited many of the experts connected to the Molloy University community to help us reshape a classroom management manuscript inclusive of current cutting-edge and research-based classroom practices that focus on enhancing student learning.

Why classroom management? Why now? The need to support educators with evidence-based practices to help manage learning was a common thread in the feedback we received from Molloy University alumni. The current teacher preparation curriculum does not afford a separate course on classroom management or cognition and learning. Therefore, this book serves to fill the gaps in addressing these needs. Furthermore, the pause in learning and instructional delivery that resulted from the pandemic called for a comprehensive reassessment of traditional classroom practices.

Before embarking on the journey to produce this book, we discussed what classroom management meant to us. Neither one of us liked the term because it resounded with prior biases of the need to "manage" students' behavior and it only hinted at what it truly means to run a classroom and shape an environment for learning. Classroom management is definitely not a term that is unidimensional. We pulled through the layers of what should be included and placed heavy emphasis on awareness of different students, learning approaches, and motivation.

In our two classroom management books, we steered away from classroom behavior management and instead focused on teachers' ability to facilitate learning, rethinking their own way of viewing students as individual entities and calibrating expectations to help students meet their learning goals. The final product was a culmination of all these elements and circled back to why teachers are in the classroom in the first place, which is to create and facilitate a learning environment.

We echo the sentiments of Dr. Alfie Kohn (1996, 2021), who emphasized the need to steer away from the "managing" aspect of the classroom to focus on engaging and responding to student needs. While a more systemic change needs to happen in the classroom to rethink curriculum and pedagogical approaches, our work, presented in both *Engaging Diverse Learners* and *Student-Centered Classrooms,* and approaches to classroom management, focus on the strategies and solutions supporting diverse learners from the perspective of growth mindset, self-regulation, mindfulness, or social-emotional learning.

Both books are anchored in the Culturally Responsive-Sustaining Education Framework, which was adapted by New York State in 2019 and aims to assist educators in creating student-centered learning environments that "affirm racial, linguistic and cultural identities; prepare students for rigor and independent learning, develop students' abilities to connect across lines of difference; elevate historically marginalized voices; and empower students as agents of social change" (New York State Education Department, 2019).

The ever-changing makeup of the twenty-first century classroom includes students who bring their diverse perspectives, experiences, and backgrounds to the forefront of who they are as students. These classrooms provide great opportunities for teachers to engage students with one another in the process of learning and capitalize on each student's unique gifts.

Our focus on diversity and equity challenged us to find a diverse set of authors who are experts in their field. We gathered authors such as educational researchers, teacher educators, behavioral experts, social workers, and mental health clinicians. Our authors also included seasoned practitioners as well as current doctoral candidates and recent alumni of the Educational Leadership Program for Diverse Learning Communities.

The *Enhanced Approaches* to classroom management, which we introduce in this book, are shaped with preservice and novice teachers in mind. It is also a welcomed introduction to current practices for in-service teachers who are seeking a refresher on classroom management. The focus of the book is to highlight proactive strategies that are often embraced by master practitioners.

In a recent research article, Rebekka Stahnke and Sigrid Blömeke (2021) discussed the different ways that novice and expert teachers approach classroom management. They found that novice teachers have a narrower perspective on classroom management and focus more on the parts rather than the whole. This finding aligns with prior research showing that novice teachers need to acclimate to their new role before they can fully connect all their skills to the needs of their students.

Novice teachers are more reactionary to students' behavior as they gain awareness of their own emotions and how their emotions impact the behavior of students. It leads them to rely more on routines and consequences with their main focus on correcting behavior rather than attempting to uncover and understand the root of behavior. Novice teachers spend energy on establishing their own authority in the classroom and focus less on student autonomy.

To help new teachers grow in their awareness of self and the needs of their students within the classroom setting, we organized the Enhanced Approaches to holistically address different dimensions of classroom management that would focus more on *proactive* strategies of student engagement and less on the *reactive* managing of behavior.

Chapter 2, "Motivating Students for Classroom Engagement," opens with content on motivating students for classroom engagement. In this chapter, two college professors with expertise in educational psychology and cognitive science explore how fostering motivation can enhance classroom structure and student behavior.

Using three key elements, the authors use the current research to define (a) how to build student-teacher relationships, (b) how to build supportive learning environments from the perspective of expectations and values attached to the learning task, and (c) how to empower students to be in charge of their own learning. The authors weave in theories such as self-determination theory, achievement goal theory, and self-regulation of learning to help educators with specific strategies to promote intrinsic motivation in their classrooms.

Chapter 3, "Fostering Relationships, Engagement, and Community to Enhance Classroom Management," focuses on the roles of relationships, engagement, and community in student learning. A seasoned elementary school teacher, a middle school district administrator, and the director of field placement at Molloy University come together to share their collective expertise on classroom management in terms of fostering connections with students. They present and discuss current ideas on building learning communities of students, teachers, and administrators.

From the elementary teacher's perspective, a classroom teacher must acknowledge the importance of his or her role as the underpinning of a child's future career in school, the one who takes the time to "hear every child's voice" and fosters the students' awareness of their membership in the school community.

The school district administrator's perspective focuses on the need to establish and maintain district-wide policies that "cultivate constructive relationships" where students, teachers, and administrators engage in meaningful, restorative practices to discuss and/or resolve classroom-wide/district-wide issues, problems, or unusual experiences.

The higher education perspective includes the responsibilities of certification-bearing programs to ensure that teacher candidates have had rich opportunities to explore the professional demands of student engagement through an unbiased acceptance of all kinds of diverse learners.

Chapter 4, "Creating Personalized Learning in Diverse Classrooms," focuses on creating personalized learning in diverse classrooms. Both authors are former educators, district administrators, and coteaching partners at Molloy University. Their chapter focuses on the positive impact of personalized learning as a classroom management approach. These authors guide readers from theory to practice as they design student-centered learning environments anchored in and supported by current research.

Using the Molloy University Lesson Plan, these authors discuss and model applications of the Understanding by Design Framework, the Universal Design for Learning Framework, and the personalized learning details of differentiation of instruction to create challenging units of study for diverse students. This chapter wraps up with a discussion on coteaching and how effectively this teaching model facilitates these frameworks and fosters student engagement.

Chapter 5, "Creating Classrooms for Culturally and Linguistically Diverse Learners," focuses on essential classroom strategies for culturally and linguistically diverse learners. The lead author is a nationally recognized expert and presenter in the area of culturally responsive teaching practices. This chapter focuses on the importance of the classroom environment as "a place to affirm, value, and use cultural identities" for teaching and learning. The authors open this chapter with a rich discussion of the historical-cultural perspectives of education in the United States and the impact of population shifts over the years on classroom management.

Using current research, the authors then analyze the data presented to inform teaching and learning through the effective implementation of asset-based approaches to build capacity for all students. By providing readers with self-reflection questions and relevant suggestions for practice, the authors guide teachers to a meaningful approach to building culturally responsive classrooms.

Chapter 6, "Communication Strategies Supporting Students for Grade-Level Transitions," explores the importance of proactive communication strategies as tools for successful classroom management. In particular, the author focuses on the effective implementation and practice of communication strategies when addressing transitions throughout students' K–12 educational journey. This chapter postulates that communication is at the heart of education and can help address the socio-emotional development of students as they face new demands in their educational journey. To support classroom teachers in accomplishing this task, the author identifies and comprehensively explains five communication strategies that serve to prioritize relationship building so that students feel safe to explore the new possibilities at all grade levels. The following section of this chapter presents a rich discussion on communication as praxis, the transformative process, whereby theory becomes practice.

The author brings this chapter to conclusion by reaffirming that students' ultimate success is dependent on the valuable contributions from educators of all grade levels and that effective communication is the conduit through which all contributions are shared and synthesized.

Chapter 7, "Fostering Social-Emotional Learning (SEL) for Classroom Management," addresses a current area of significant concern in the field of education: students' social-emotional regulation. This chapter discusses social-emotional regulation through the lens of mental health. Two professors/practitioners of social work and a counseling expert shared their insights on this topic. Throughout this chapter, the authors highlight the effectiveness of addressing social-emotional regulation through the implementation of interventions anchored in developmental approaches with a social justice perspective.

Since classroom teachers are often the first to identify students struggling with social-emotional issues, our authors also address the critical importance of open and interactive collaboration among professional staff in school communities. While the authors maintain their focus on classroom interventions in this chapter, they do encourage school personnel to connect with families and community resources.

This chapter is masterfully organized to address social-emotional regulation at specific developmental levels and in specific academic settings. Through the authors' effective use of charts and vignettes to support text, readers can easily identify behaviors of concerns and effective classroom strategies as well as make professional connections to other chapters in this book.

REFERENCES

Alcruz, J., & Blair, M. A. (Eds.). (2022). *Student-centered classrooms: Research-driven and inclusive strategies for classroom management.* Rowman & Littlefield.

Kohn, A. (1996). *Beyond discipline: From compliance to community.* Association for Supervision & Curriculum Development.

Kohn, A. (2021). The classroom-management field can't stop chasing the wrong goal: When will we stop trying to 'manage' children? *Education Week*, September 17. Retrieved from https://www.edweek.org/teaching-learning/opinion-the-classroom-management-field-cant-stop-chasing-the-wrong-goal/2021/09.

New York State Education Department. (2019). *Culturally responsive-sustaining education.* Retrieved on 05/05/2022 from http://www.nysed.gov/curriculum-instruction/culturally-responsive-sustaining-education-framework.

Stahnke, R., & Blömeke, S. (2021). Novice and expert teachers' situation-specific skills regarding classroom management: What do they perceive, interpret and suggest? *Teaching and Teacher Education, 98, 103243.* https://doi.org/10.1016/j.tate.2020.103243.

Motivating Students for Classroom Engagement

Joanna Alcruz and Mubina Schroeder

> Success is not final; failure is not fatal: It is the courage to continue that counts.
>
> —Winston S. Churchill

If you practice martial arts and your goal is to acquire a black belt, which option would help you accomplish it? Option 1 starts with motivation to meet the goal, which leads to action (of practice) and follows with results (black belt). Option 2 begins with action, brings the results, and leads to motivation. If you choose Option 1 and your results are not satisfactory—especially early on when learning and working toward the goal—motivation may quickly fade away and so may the goal. Option 2 is more promising, as action leads to motivation and propels more action. Small successes can sustain motivation, and the results, even if not initially satisfactory, can still ignite action to correct it and fuel motivation.

The purpose of this chapter is to examine different motivational approaches to help students become motivated and engage with the content, leading to the improvement of their classroom behavior as a result. The role of the teacher in this process is essential, as the interactions and feedback they offer to students can either place them in a position of defeat or encourage them to overcome the obstacles they face.

From the past perspective of classroom management, motivation has been applied from the behavioral "carrot and stick" approach. However, this chapter proposes to shift the focus to finding "what makes students tick" and helping them uncover learning potentials that will also help to redirect attention and behavior to productive classroom outcomes. The question then is no longer *if* and *when* the students can get the black belt but *how* the students can focus on the skills that will get them there.

DEFINITIONS OF *MOTIVATION*

Depending on the theoretical perspective, the definition of *motivation* can highlight a different focus. Motivation is a theoretical construct used to explain the initiation, direction, intensity, persistence, and quality of behavior, especially goal-directed behavior (Maehr & Meyer, 1997). At the same time, it is more of a process than an outcome. Rather than a general trait, motivation is considered to be situated and changeable as a function of instruction tasks and activities that take place in a classroom. Therefore, it is important to not classify students as being "more" or "less" motivated, as that can change from situation to situation. What counts is the quality of student engagement.

Behaviorists, such as Skinner (1976), view motivation as schedules of positive and negative reinforcements. Here, the positive feedback as reinforcement leads to good grades, while negative or no feedback, under the same circumstances, can hinder grades. The concept of *reward and punishment* has long been applied in classroom management to control student behavior. It can still be seen through the application of popular tools in educational settings such as *Classroom Dojo* (www.classdojo.com) or *Positive Behavior Interventions and Supports* (www.pbis.org). However, one of the criticisms of the behaviorist approach to motivating students is that in the process of controlling behavior through rewards and punishments, students' autonomy of choice is often eliminated (Kohn, 1996, 2021). The research on using awards to motivate complex behavior actually leads to adverse reactions, where the motivation decreases as the reward increases (Jovanovic & Matejevic, 2014).

The cognitive view of motivation shifts from the extrinsic behavior control to more intrinsic drive guiding the choices that result in action. An active processing of information can place learners in a position of recognizing that their current knowledge and beliefs might be insufficient or incomplete. This recognition calls upon the learners to restructure their current cognitive structures, which can only be accomplished with personal investment that comes from within (Perry, 1999; Ryan & Deci, 2006).

The cognitive motivation espouses concepts such as (a) expectancy-value theory, which focuses on the expectations of outcomes and the importance that students place on the outcome (Wigfield & Eccles, 2000), and (b) attribution theory, which looks at how learners attribute or judge the outcomes of behavior, due to either internal dispositions or external circumstances (Graham & Weiner, 2012; Harvey & Martinko, 2009; Weiner, 2018).

The social cognitive theory focuses on the interplay and reciprocal interactions of behavioral, personal, and environmental factors as proposed by Albert Bandura (1977, 1986), where social environment plays a critical role in aspects like motivation, learning, or self-regulation (Schunk & Usher,

2019). Motivation is presented here as processes that support and sustain goal-directed behavior. These processes can encompass aspects such as "choice, effort, persistence, achievement, and environmental regulation" (Schunk & DiBenedetto, 2020), with the current emphasis on agency.

Self-efficacy beliefs, the main drivers of motivated action, refer to individuals' belief in their ability to perform or produce a specific skill (Bandura 1977, 1997) and reflect one's confidence in the ability to control one's own motivation, behavior, and social environment. They can differ depending on the content (subject matter) or the context (circumstances related to the occurrence of behavior).

The last definition we would like to mention comes from self-determination theory. Ryan and Deci (2000) focused on motivation based on not only the quantity but also the quality, including type and orientation. The authors proposed the *intrinsic and extrinsic view of motivation*, which is not binary in nature but rather serves as a continuum of how motivation evolves from one spectrum to another (see figure 2.1).

Extrinsic motivation is a drive to act based on the incentives or punishments related to the task performed, while *intrinsic motivation* is driven by personal enjoyment of the task (Ryan & Deci, 2000). The shift from external to internal factors that propel students to act (or not) can start with the total lack of motivation (amotivation), shifting to extrinsic motivation phases of External Regulation and Introjection and then moving to more autonomous

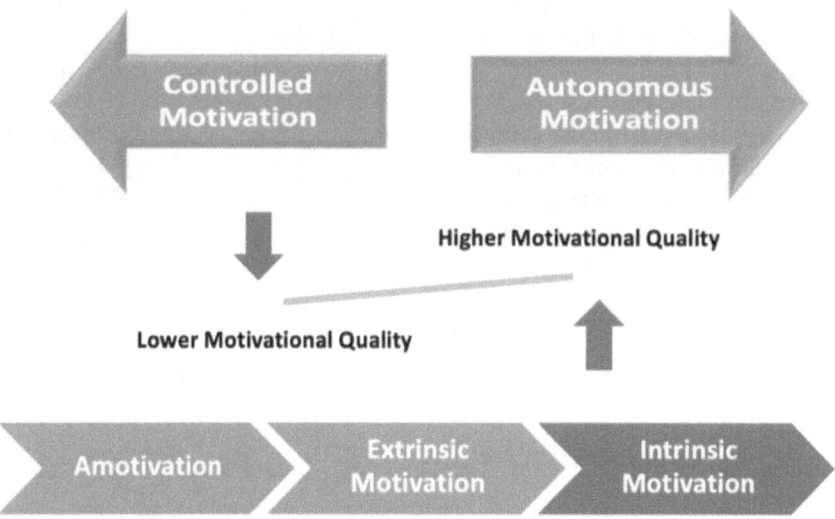

Figure 2.1. Self-determination theory dimensions.
Source: Adapted from Ryan and Deci (2000).

and internal phases of Identification and Integration, which, when achieved, will turn into Intrinsic Motivation (Niemiec & Ryan, 2009).

In any conversation about motivating students, it is important to remember that motivation is not a fixed state that transfers from one task or subject to another. Rather, it is both context and circumstance dependent, where the student learning environment can either enhance or diminish their motivation to act.

How Is Motivation Related to Classroom Management?

Classroom management calls for teachers to produce a set of processes and rules that will allow for a safe and nurturing environment suitable for learning and appropriate student behavior. With this in mind, the motivation of the teachers and the students can enhance the process of learning and build a classroom culture where behavioral discord can be kept to a minimum.

The direction of classroom management has begun to take a turn from managing classrooms and behavioral approaches to building caring learning communities within classroom and school settings. The role of the student as a passive recipient of knowledge (teacher-centered approach) is now replaced with giving students opportunities to actively partake and shape their learning experiences (student-centered approach).

The concept of *autonomy support*, which came from self-determination theory (Ryan & Deci, 2000), emphasizes the need for every individual to experience a sense of agency. Research on the topic has shown that autonomy support benefits students' motivation to learn, well-being, and academic outcomes (e.g., Evans & Boucher, 2015; Furtak & Kunter, 2012).

Student agency in the classroom can include examples such as co-creating classroom rules, co-constructing elements of the assignment rubrics, or having options to choose meaningful learning activities. However, research also indicates that teachers are not always ready or are resistant to having classrooms where students co-create their learning environment (Evans & Boucher, 2015; Furtak & Kunter, 2012).

The concept of *teacher self-efficacy* refers to teachers' perceptions of their own abilities to help students (Morris et al., 2017; Zee & Koomen, 2016). Teachers with higher self-efficacy are more willing and persistent when helping students or engaging them in challenging tasks. Although the reciprocal nature of influence between students and teachers from the self-efficacy perspective calls for more attention, the current findings on the positive relationship between self-efficacy and student outcomes are promising (e.g., Holzberger et al., 2013; Klassen et al., 2011).

Following the words of Alfie Kohn (2021), an expert on classroom management, it is important to shift thinking from asking, "How can I get these kids to do what I tell them?" to "What do these kids need? How can I help them to meet those needs?" (para. 12).

KEY ASPECTS TO BUILDING AND SUSTAINING STUDENT MOTIVATION TO LEARN

Building Relationships

One of the fundamental steps of cultivating motivation and enhancing classroom management is to build positive teacher-student relationships. Students who feel that the teacher is not only there to guide and critique their work but also to care for who they are and what they want to accomplish will be more open to learning and less susceptible to behavioral outbursts.

Students' basic needs for relatedness and the sense of belonging in classroom settings are directly related to their feelings that the teacher cares for them. Teacher expressions of genuine liking of the students, respect of who the students are, and valuing them as individuals further promote positive relationships between students and teachers and their sense of connectedness.

From the classroom management perspective and in the spirit of self-determination theory, this sense of belonging and being part of the classroom can help students "internalize and accept as their own the values and practices of those to whom they feel, or want to feel, connected" (Niemiec & Ryan, 2009, p. 139). With the process of internalization, students can adapt easily to the structure of the classroom. There are numerous studies highlighting that when the basic needs for autonomy and belonging are met within the classroom setting, students tend to do better academically and feel more satisfied about their learning (e.g., Allen et al., 2021; Jang et al., 2009).

The classroom management style espoused by the teacher has ramifications for the extent and quality of student-teacher interactions. Adapted from the work of Baumrind (1971) on parental styles, classroom management styles look at the degree of teacher involvement and classroom regulation. The three styles included in this discussion are (a) permissive, (b) authoritarian, and (c) authoritative.

When teachers adapt a permissive style of managing the classroom, they typically display minimal involvement with students and minimal classroom regulation. The classroom structure has only a few demands on students and no consequences for their actions. With too much freedom and not enough structure, students can have difficulties regulating their behavior.

When teachers embrace an authoritarian management approach, they also show a low degree of involvement with students but a high degree of classroom regulation. This classroom structure brings many demands and behavioral rules on the students that are often restrictive and punitive in nature. The motivation of students will be driven by the fear of consequences and can lead to behavioral outbursts.

The most beneficial approach that promotes positive relationships between the students and teachers, and motivates students to learn, is reflected by the authoritative style to classroom management. Here, teachers show a high degree of involvement and a high degree of classroom regulation. The warm and caring approach is paired with high and clear expectations for behavior. Provided with classroom structure and nurturing support, students tend to flourish both academically and behaviorally.

Building a Supportive Learning Environment

To promote motivation through which students generate, direct, and sustain their behavior toward learning, it is important to consider two core aspects of motivation that include (a) expectancies related to learning outcomes and (b) values attached to those outcomes (Atkinson, 1957; Vroom, 1964; Wigfield & Eccles, 2000). The supportive environment is the fertile ground where those learning outcomes can be realized.

Expectancies related to learning outcomes

The question of "Can I do the task?" guides students' expectancies or expectations toward the task and final outcome. The theories that support the concept of expectancies include self-concept, self-esteem, and self-efficacy. A brief description of each is included in figure 2.2.

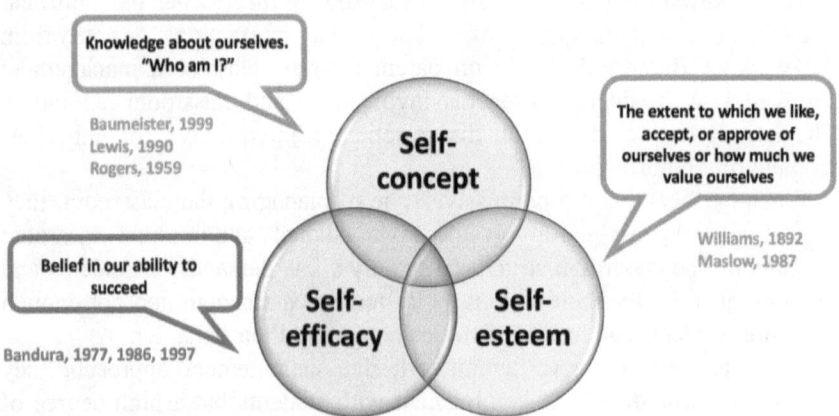

Figure 2.2. Motivational theories related to expectancy.

One way of building students' view of self and their work is through constructive feedback. Studies of effective teaching and learning (Dinham, 2007; Nash & Winstone, 2017) have shown that learners want to know where they stand in regard to their work. It is important to note that younger students are not always ready to receive negative feedback about their work. They often perceive it from a whole-person perspective. They tend to think that they failed as a person rather than failed the task at hand. One deals with the self-concept, while the other with self-efficacy. Helping students understand the difference and teaching them how to receive feedback can make a long-lasting difference.

The expectancy theories primarily differ in terms of level of specificity, with self-concept and self-esteem being more global and self-efficacy being more task- or domain-driven. When self-efficacy and self-concept beliefs are assessed at the same level of specificity (such as the domain level of geography), they tend to predict achievement equally well. But when efficacy is assessed at the task-specific level, it is a stronger predictor of achievement than self-concept. Research suggests that it is easier to change individuals' self-efficacy beliefs than self-concept (Bong & Clark, 1999). Therefore, helping students enhance their "can do" attitude toward a specific task can also result in greater success at accomplishing them.

Another theory closely related to students' expectancy of task is Carol Dweck's (2008) Growth Mindset theory. Students will often struggle with learning when, in their minds, the task is overwhelming or too difficult. They may also think that the task is beyond their ability and only "smarter" people can do it. The latter aspect illustrates the fixed growth mindset, where students perceive their abilities and intelligence as something that cannot be changed. On the other hand, students who espouse the growth mindset believe that through effort, hard work, good strategies, and feedback from others, their abilities can be further developed (Dweck, 2008).

A growth mindset can drive both motivation and achievement. When students believe they can get smarter, they will simultaneously make learning their goal and look at effort as an opportunity to make them stronger. This will result in students spending more time learning and working harder to accomplish their learning goals, leading to higher academic achievement (Blackwell et al., 2007). Helping students make a leap from a fixed mindset to a growth mindset would also be helping them see that their specific actions related to learning will also get them closer to accomplishing positive outcomes.

Another powerful and overlapping phenomenon to mindset that can influence learning is stereotype threat; this is when an individual feels compelled to confirm or corroborate a stereotype associated with the racial, ethnic, gender, or cultural group that the individual is a member of (Steele & Aronson, 1995). Unfortunately, research has shown that negative stereotypes can prime individuals to perform more poorly on standardized tests, behave negatively, and have poorer outcomes. For example, even minor reminders of group membership, such as asking students what their race is before an exam, can have an impact on student performance (Shapiro, 2011).

Values related to learning outcomes

Shifting now from expectancies about the task to the values related to the task, the main guiding question is, "Do I want to do this activity and why?" So often, students ask, "Why do I have to learn or do this?" It all relates to students' own assessments of the task and whether they feel it is important, interesting, or somehow useful to them. Helping students realize the importance of the task and its utility can help them recognize the value in it. If teachers do not pause and spend time helping students make the connection between the task at hand and its importance, they can miss a great opportunity to motivate their students.

The learning outcomes and objectives that guide the lesson activities and assessments serve as learning goals for the teacher and students. However, these goals can hold different meanings to different students depending on the value and importance they attach to a given task or learning experience. Some students may want to learn for the sake of understanding, which is known as mastery approach. Others may care more about showing that they are better than other students, known as performance approach. And there are also students in the middle, who just want to get by.

The values related to the tasks can translate into different types of goals that students have. Some goals can relate to the *cost value*, whether it be time, money, or positive/negative experiences attached to learning. The *extrinsic value* goals are driven by external factors, like praise, grade, or recognition, while the *intrinsic value* goals include focus on the satisfaction of engaging in the process of doing the task but not necessarily the outcome. There are also *attainment value* goals, which include both mastery as well as successful completion of the task. Helping students realize what value they place on a learning outcome can help them to meet those goals.

The achievement goal theories aim to measure student achievement motivation (Dweck, 1986; Elliot, 1999; Nicholls, 1984, 1989). The original dichotomous approach considered only the level of competency (Elliot, 1999; Nicholls, 1984). However, as the theory evolved, the dimension of valance was added with the approach (positive) and avoidance (negative) tendencies (Elliot & Covington, 2001).

In figure 2.3, the distinction of a 2×2 achievement goal model is defined (Elliot & McGregor, 2001). In the most current rendition of goal theory, a 3×2 model accounts for (in greater precision) the task-based, intra- and

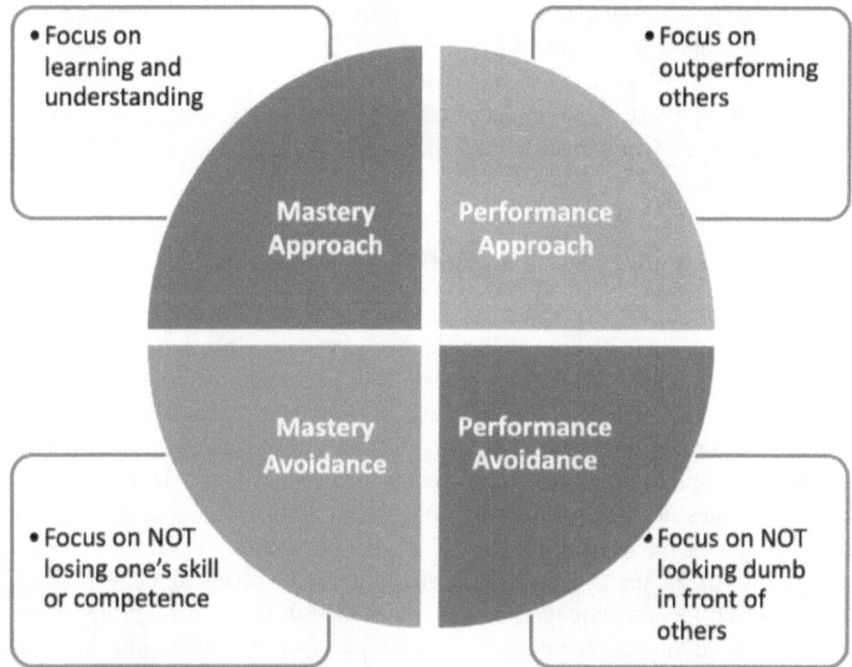

Figure 2.3. 2 × 2 achievement goal model.
Source: Adapted from Elliot and McGregor (2001).

interpersonal standards that guide student decisions and motivation. In this latest model, mastery goals can have task-approach, task-avoidance, self-approach, and self-avoidance, while performance goals look at other-approach and other-avoidance.

An understanding of where the students are in terms of their achievement goal orientation can shed more light on where students place their value on the task and how their motivation can be further enhanced. In the classroom context, teachers can also present different goal structures that can enhance or be more detrimental to student motivation.

Ames (1984, 1992) described three different classroom structures and potential outcomes related to them:

- *Competitive structures*—More successful students are set against less successful students in attaining the goal. In the process of competition, only a few students will reach the goal successfully.
- *Cooperative structures*—Students are placed in groups and, as members, share successes and failures of the group. In this process, students are winning or failing together as a group.

- *Individualistic structures*—Each student is rated based on individual performance, independent of others.

Considering those different goal-related theories, the classroom context can predetermine whether students will be more willing to adopt performance or mastery goals.

Helping Students Be in Charge of Their Own Learning

Students often face challenging tasks, which can lead them to thinking that the task is too difficult or that the teacher gave poor instructions for them to complete the task. Without proper tools and encouragement, students can resign themselves to the state of helplessness and choose to blame internal or external factors for their lack of success. So, what can teachers do to help shift students' thinking to the point of empowerment rather than defeat?

Cultivating students to begin relying on themselves to gauge many aspects of learning is at the heart of the theory of Self-Regulation of Learning (SRL). According to Zimmerman (2000), SRL refers to students' beliefs about their own abilities to engage and pursue academic goals through appropriate actions, thoughts, feelings, and behaviors, while self-monitoring and reflecting on the learning progress they are making toward the completion of their goal.

The current models of SRL include both meta-cognitive and regulatory dimensions that focus on self-monitoring, with direct links to motivation (Dinsmore et al., 2008; Greene, 2018; Schunk & Zimmerman, 2008). SRL skills may increase over time and can be taught or enhanced through direct instruction, modeling, support, and classroom organization and structure. Students who develop into self-regulated learners tend to be meta-cognitively, motivationally, and behaviorally proactive in their learning and in achieving their learning goals.

The Cyclical Phases Model of SRL (Zimmerman & Moylan, 2009) has three key phases, as shown in figure 2.4:

a. **Forethought**, which is focused on determining the value of the task and a student's self-motivation to pursue it;
b. **Performance**, which is focused on gauging task-related self-control and self-observation of task-driven actions; and
c. **Self-reflection**, which is focused on a student's ability to assess, judge, and make corrective actions based on the outcome of the task.

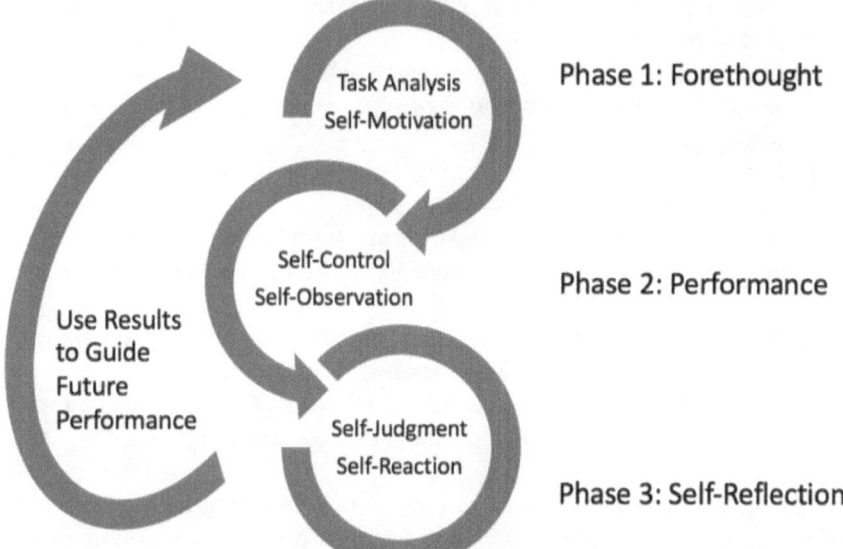

Figure 2.4. Self-regulated learning model.
Source: Adapted from Zimmerman (2000) and Zimmerman and Moylan (2009).

SRL comprises three aspects: (a) cognition, (b) meta-cognition, and (c) motivation. The first component of SRL includes *cognition*, which focuses on the skills and habits necessary to encode, memorize, and recall information. The cognition component includes three types of learning skills: (a) strategies to learn, (b) problem solving, and (c) critical thinking.

This area can be a fertile ground for teachers to introduce students to various learning techniques and approaches that might be specific to a given content. How students will be learning statistics is very different from learning history or essay composition. Therefore, it is important to introduce students early on to more high-utility learning strategies that require a bit of training but bring much higher results in terms of recall or understanding of new concepts.

Although most commonly used learning strategies tend to be dominated by highlighting, outlining the chapters, or rereading the material, shifting students to applying visual representation or formulating questions through the process of learning can be more impactful. The high-utility learning strategies compiled by a group of cognitive psychological researchers under the platform of The Learning Scientists (www.learningscientists.org) present six research-supported learning approaches:

1. **Spaced practice**—Spacing studying sessions over time and allowing time to process information
2. **Elaboration**—Including many details when describing and explaining ideas and forming connections between concepts to explain how they work together
3. **Concrete examples**—Illustrating learning with specific examples to build understanding of abstract concepts
4. **Interleaving**—Switching ideas during studying session and breaking up the order in which they were introduced to strengthen the understanding (e.g., ABC, BCA, CAB)
5. **Retrieval practice**—Practice bringing information to mind through tools such as practice quizzes, detailed flashcards, etc.
6. **Dual coding**—Combining words and visuals or forming visual representations like concept maps, timelines, and cartoon strips

The next aspect of SRL is *meta-cognition*, or thinking about one's own thinking. It includes students' awareness of their own cognition (monitoring) and their ability to regulate their cognitive processes depending on the context (control). For example, a student spent many hours studying for the test and felt very prepared, only to find a poor result. The meta-cognitive awareness here was not fully accurate. By using one's own reflection about the failed test, students can guide their response to it, exemplifying the control process.

In their book *Connect the Dots*, Taylor and Dibner (2019) presented several strategies that can help students form a more accurate meta-cognitive awareness of their own thinking:

1. **Modeling**—Giving examples of meta-cognitive thinking while working through a task or a problem
2. **Explicit instruction**—Embedding meta-cognitive instruction into content areas and assignments, rather than separating it as a "study skill"
3. **Verbalization**—Including meta-cognitive talk as part of teaching and encouraging students to express it in a safe and encouraging classroom setting
4. **Self-talk**—Including self-talk strategies to help students cope with difficulties that would assist them in reframing their thinking, adjusting attitude, and regulating their emotions

Another strategy of building meta-cognitive awareness in students is helping them form a habit of asking question to monitor own progress. With every lesson or challenging task, they can ask themselves the following questions (adapted from Retrievalpractice.org):

- What are three things I have learned in this class, module, etc.?
- What questions do I have about this content or need clarification on?
- What ideas or concepts do I confidently understand?

SRL is also directly connected to *motivation*—specifically, the self-efficacy element of it (the confidence to perform a task or accomplish a goal; Bandura, 1977) as well as epistemological beliefs (the origin and nature of knowledge). As discussed earlier, some other strategies to support motivation include appropriate goal setting and self-monitoring.

One additional dimension that enhances motivation in students includes specific progress feedback. Maintaining high standards and high structured support for students to accomplish their learning outcomes can offset the students' low view of self. How teachers choose to guide their students through the productive struggles can shape their perseverance or lack thereof.

Effective feedback for learning goes beyond adding smiley faces or comments like "excellent" or "great." For feedback to be productive, it needs to be focused on specific skills or understanding that students are working on and developing. While highlighting the areas for improvement, teachers should also offer strategies and resources to address the gaps.

Anchoring feedback in the standards, rather than personal bias or perceptions that the teacher may hold about individual students, can alleviate negative views held by students (Yeager et al., 2014). Paired with positive encouragement, the structured support and resources can provide the environment for all students to succeed. Even small academic victories can begin to motivate students to work more and harder toward their learning goals.

STRATEGIES TO ENGAGE AND MOTIVATE DIVERSE STUDENTS AND LEARNERS

In this section of exploring motivation, the focus is on strategies that teachers can apply in classroom settings. Strategies are examined from the perspective of sustaining motivation as well as promoting intrinsic levels of motivation.

Teacher Expectations

The earlier discussion was on how students perceive themselves and their ability to complete a task successfully in the context of self-concept, self-esteem, and self-efficacy. It is not only that educators build the capacity for students to believe in themselves but also that they believe that students can meet high standards.

The APA standard 11 states, "Teachers' expectations about their students affect students' opportunities to learn, their motivation and their learning outcomes" (American Psychological Association, Coalition for Psychology in Schools and Education, 2015, p. 19). This is connected to potential biases and stereotypes that make them self-fulfilling prophecies (Jussim & Harber, 2005).

The seminal study on "Pygmalion in the Classroom" by Rosenthal and Jacobson (1968) evidenced that teacher expectations can significantly affect student achievement. If faulty expectations are communicated to students, they may begin to perform in ways that confirm the teacher's original expectation. When these inaccurate expectations occur, they are more likely to be directed toward stigmatized groups such as ethnic minorities, economically disadvantaged students, LGBTQ+ students, and so forth.

A meta-analysis study on teacher expectations (Tenenbaum & Ruck, 2007) found that teachers held higher expectations for Asian American students and provided more positive interactions for European American children than Black or Latino/a children. In another study, in classrooms where teachers held implicit negative attitudes toward certain ethnic groups, the students in those groups performed poorly when compared to other peers (van den Bergh et al., 2010).

A recent study that focused on roles of motivation, race, and faculty on fostering academic achievement (Roksa et al., 2020) highlighted that when faculty did not express much interest in student learning, the academic motivation of White students persevered but diminished for African American students.

Teacher expectations can translate into behaviors that affect student performance and contribute to a classroom climate in which equality can be significantly compromised. Therefore, monitoring one's own prejudices and biases can be a strategy to prevent the Pygmalion effect in the classroom. Another approach can be to hold the "high standards, high support" strategy for all students.

Those who experience challenges while learning can still meet the standards with proper scaffolding and guidance. Those who do not experience the same challenges when learning can be challenged to explore more advanced content and be guided through that process. In both examples, students are surrounded by affirmation and support that can help them stay motivated and on task.

Key Aspects to Promote Intrinsic Motivation

This chapter introduced and offered different strategies around student engagement and motivation. The pursuit of learning for the sake of learning is directly connected with mastery goal orientation and intrinsic motivation. Fostering those higher motivational aspirations among students leads to higher academic outcomes (Zlate & Cucui, 2015). Yet, it is important to recognize, as Ryan and Deci (2006) pointed out in their Self-Determination Theory, that motivation is a continuum, and in order to get to intrinsic motivation, students often need to go through the phases of extrinsic motivation.

To develop good habits in students, which, if formed well, can serve them throughout their learning journey (Fiorella, 2020), an emphasis on extrinsic motivation can be beneficial. Promoting extrinsic motivation can be instrumental when the level of initial interest may be low or when students are developing skills that require repetition and practice (Deci et al., 2001). Once the skill is mastered, the confidence level of students typically increases and their motivation transitions from the extrinsic to the intrinsic side of the continuum.

Table 2.1 summarizes the key strategies that teachers can apply to promote the development of intrinsic motivation.

CONCLUSION

The importance of motivation in the classroom cannot be emphasized enough. Research has consistently shown that student motivation is directly related to success in learning outcomes. However, increasing student motivation remains a perennial frustration for many teachers and schools; the key is to understand how to elicit and maintain motivation in students by utilizing insights on mindset, self-regulation skills, and resilience.

Today, many teachers use motivational strategies in the classroom but tend to focus on extrinsic motivators such as rewards or prizes for grades and good behaviors. As discussed in this chapter, the more crucial element of motivation that schools need to pivot to is intrinsic factors such as promoting a growth mindset (praising effort rather than outcome), teaching students self-regulated learning strategies that foster meta-cognitive thinking (which in turn leads to agency in learning), and creating an autonomy-supportive classroom culture of resilience where students understand that mistakes are an important element of learning (Kusurkar et al., 2011).

Many decades ago, teachers tended to apply harsh punishments to discourage unwanted behavior or poor performance in classrooms. While most schools have moved away from traditional punishment/reward systems, there is still much improvement to be made. Traditional punishment/reward systems are consistently associated with lower motivation and student engagement (see Moberly et al., 2005).

Table 2.1. Strategies to Promote Motivation

Motivational Strategies	What Teachers Can Do	Theory Connection
Do I have a choice? Increase students' sense of personal autonomy and self-determination in classroom	• Offer choices on assignments and activities • Co-construct rules of engagement with students • Avoid excessive extrinsic controls • Limit the public recognition of individual students' work to avoid engendering a sense of competition or shaming	Self-Determination Theory
Do I want to do it? Promote the sense of curiosity	• Connect learning to what students know, want to know, and need to know • Place learning in meaningful and exciting contexts • Illustrate the inherent utility of the content • Personalize the instruction to the interests of students	Expectancy-Value Theory
Can I do it? Promote a sense of expectancy	• Emphasize the importance of productive struggle • Emphasize how failure can be an opportunity for growth • Encourage the view of intelligence as malleable, not fixed • Make it safe for students to take risks in exploring new strategies	Self-efficacy Growth mindset
How can I do it? Encourage learning goals	• Model specific steps that will lead to desired outcomes • Sequence tasks with appropriate levels of challenge	Achievement Goal Theories Self-Regulated Learning
How can I get support to do it? Create challenging learning environments with high support	• Use various modes of learning delivery • Use technology to promote and enhance learning • Use peer support and tutors • Set up opportunities for cooperative learning	High-Utility Strategies
How can I do it better next time? Promote self-reflection	• Give high-quality, wise feedback • Engage learners in acknowledging their learning through self-evaluation and self-reflection • Acknowledge learning to learn as a skill	Self-Regulated Learning Metacognition

Schools should embrace practices such as mindfulness and reflection as alternatives to punishment (Li et al., 2019), even if this shift means dismantling conventional and long-established classroom culture. As stakeholders in education, we have an obligation to use educational research insights to create the right classroom supports for students.

REFERENCES

Allen, K. A., Slaten, C. D., Arslan, G., Roffey, S., Craig, H., Vella-Brodrick, D. A. (2021). School belonging: The importance of student and teacher relationships. In M. L. Kern, & M. L. Wehmeyer, (Eds.) *The Palgrave handbook of positive education*. Palgrave Macmillan, Cham. https://doi.org/10.1007/978-3-030-64537-3_21.

American Psychological Association, Coalition for Psychology in Schools and Education. (2015). *Top 20 principles from psychology for preK–12 teaching and learning*. Retrieved from http://www.apa.org/ed/schools/cpse/top-twenty-principles.pdf.

Ames, C. (1984). Competitive, cooperative and individualistic goal structure: A cognitive-motivational analysis. In R. Ames (Ed.), *Research on motivation in education* (Vol. 1, pp. 177–207). Academic Press.

Ames, C. (1992). Classrooms: Goals, structure, and student motivation. *Journal of Educational Psychology, 84*, 261–71.

Atkinson, J. W. (1957). Motivational determinants of risk-taking behavior. *Psychological Review, 64*(6, Pt. 1), 359–72. https://doi.org/10.1037/h0043445.

Bandura, A. (1977). Self-efficacy: Toward a unifying theory of behavioral change. *Psychological Review, 84*(2), 191–215.

Bandura, A. (1986). *Social foundations of thought and action: A social cognitive theory*. Prentice-Hall.

Bandura, A. (1997). *Self-efficacy: The exercise of control*. W. H. Freeman.

Baumrind, D. (1971). Current patterns of parental authority. *Developmental Psychology Monograph, 4*, 1–103. http://dx.doi.org/10.1037/h0030372.

Blackwell, L. S., Trzesniewski, K. H., & Dweck, C. S. (2007). Implicit theories of intelligence predict achievement across an adolescent transition: A longitudinal study and an intervention. *Child Development, 78*(1), 246–63.

Bong, M., & Clark, R. E. (1999). Comparison between self-concept and self-efficacy in academic motivation research. *Educational Psychologist, 33*(3), 139–53. https://doi.org/10.1207/s15326985ep3403_1.

Deci, E. L., Koestner, R., & Ryan, R. M. (2001). Extrinsic rewards and intrinsic motivation in education: Reconsidered once again. *Review of Educational Research, 71*(1), 1–27. doi:10.3102/00346543071001001.

Dinham, S. (2007). How schools get moving and keep improving: Leadership for teacher learning, student success and school renewal. *Australian Journal of Education, 51*(3), 263–75.

Dinsmore, D. L., Alexander, P. A., & Loughlin, S. M. (2008). Focusing the conceptual lens on metacognition, self-regulation, and self-regulated learning. *Educational Psychology Review, 20*, 391–409. https://doi.org/10.1007/s10648-008-9083-6.

Dweck, C. S. (1986). Motivational processes affecting learning. *American Psychologist, 41*(10), 1040–48. https://doi.org/10.1037/0003-066X.41.10.1040.

Dweck, C. S. (2008). *Mindset: The new psychology of success*. Random House Digital.

Elliot, A. J. (1999). Approach and avoidance motivation and achievement goals. *Educational Psychologist, 34*(3), 169–89. https://doi.org/10.1207/s15326985ep3403_3.

Elliot, A. J., & Covington, M. V. (2001). Approach and avoidance motivation. *Educational Psychology Review, 13*(2), 73–92. https://doi.org/10.1023/A:1009009018235

Elliot, A. J., & McGregor, H. A. (2001). A 2 × 2 achievement goal framework. *Journal of Personality and Social Psychology, 80*(3), 501–19. https://doi.org/10.1037/0022-3514.80.3.501.

Evans, M., & Boucher, A. R. (2015). Optimizing the power of choice: Supporting student autonomy to foster motivation and engagement in learning. *Mind, Brain, and Education, 9*(2), 87–91.

Fiorella, L. (2020). The science of habit and its implications for student learning and well-being. *Educational Psychology Review, 32*(3), 603–25. doi:10.1007/s10648-020-09525-1.

Furtak, E. M., & Kunter, M. (2012). Effects of autonomy-supportive teaching on student learning and motivation. *Journal of Experimental Education, 80*(3), 284–316.

Graham, S., & Weiner, B. (2012). Motivation: Past, present, and future. In K. R. Harris, S. Graham, T. Urdan, C. B. McCormick, G. M. Sinatra, & J. Sweller (Eds.), APA educational psychology handbook, vol. 1. Theories, constructs, and critical issues (pp. 367–97). American Psychological Association. https://doi.org/10.1037/13273-013.

Greene, J. A. (2018). *Self-regulation in education*. Routledge.

Harvey, P., & Martinko, M. J. (2009). An empirical examination of the role of attributions in psychological entitlement and its outcomes. *Journal of Organizational Behavior, 30*, 143–58.

Holzberger, D., Philipp, A., & Kunter, M. (2013). How teachers' self-efficacy is related to instructional quality: A longitudinal analysis. Journal of Educational Psychology, 105(3), 774–86. https://doi.org/10.1037/a0032198.

Jang, H., Reeve, J., Ryan, R. M., & Kim, A. (2009). Can self-determination theory explain what underlies the productive, satisfying learning experiences of collectivistically-oriented Korean students? *Journal of Educational Psychology, 101*(3), 644–61.

Jovanovic, D., & Matejevic, M. (2014). Relationship between rewards and intrinsic motivation for learning—researches review. *Procedia—Social and Behavioral Sciences, 149*(5), 456–60. doi:10.1016/j.sbspro.2014.08.287.

Jussim, L., & Harber, K. D. (2005). Teacher expectations and self-fulfilling prophecies: Knowns and unknowns, resolved and unresolved controversies. *Personality and Social Psychology Review, 9*(2), 131–55. doi:10.1207/s15327957pspr0902_3.

Klassen, R. M., Tze, V. M. C., Betts, S. M., & Gordon, K. A. (2011). Teacher efficacy research 1998–2009: Signs of progress or unfulfilled promise? *Educational Psychology Review, 23*(1), 21–43. https://doi.org/10.1007/s10648-010-9141-8

Kohn, A. (1996). *Beyond discipline: From compliance to community*. Association for Supervision & Curriculum Development.

Kohn, A. (2021). The classroom-management field can't stop chasing the wrong goal. *Education Week*. Retrieved from https://www.edweek.org/teaching-learning/opinion-the-classroom-management-field-cant-stop-chasing-the-wrong-goal/2021/09.

Kusurkar, R. A., Croiset, G., & Ten Cate, O. T. J. (2011). Twelve tips to stimulate intrinsic motivation in students through autonomy-supportive classroom teaching derived from self-determination theory. *Medical Teacher, 33*(12), 978–82. doi: 10.3109/0142159X.2011.599896.

Li, C., Kee, Y. H., Kong, L. C., Zou, L., Ng, K. L., & Li, H. (2019). Autonomy-supportive teaching and basic psychological need satisfaction among school students: The role of mindfulness. *International Journal of Environmental Research and Public Health, 16*(14), 2599. doi: 10.3390/ijerph16142599.

Maehr, M. L., & Meyer, H. A. (1997). Understanding motivation and schooling: Where we've been, where we are, and where we need to go. *Educational Psychology Review, 9*(4), 371–409. doi:10.1023/a:1024750807365.

Moberly, D. A., Waddle, J. L., & Duff, R. E. (2005). The use of rewards and punishment in early childhood classrooms. *Journal of Early Childhood Teacher Education, 25*(4), 359–66. https://doi.org/10.1080/1090102050250410

Morris, D. B., Usher, E. L., & Chen, J. A. (2017). Reconceptualizing the sources of teaching self-efficacy: A critical review of emerging literature. *Educational Psychology Review, 29*, 795–833.

Nash, R. A., & Winstone, N. E. (2017). Responsibility-sharing in the giving and receiving of assessment feedback. *Frontiers in psychology, 8*, 1519.

Nicholls, J. G. (1984). Achievement motivation: Conceptions of ability, subjective experience, task choice, and performance. *Psychological Review, 91*(3), 328–46. https://doi.org/10.1037/0033-295X.91.3.328.

Nicholls, J. G. (1989). *The competitive ethos and democratic education*. Harvard University Press.

Niemiec, C. P., & Ryan, R. M. (2009). Autonomy, competence, and relatedness in the classroom: Applying self-determination theory to educational practice. *Theory and Research in Education, 7, 133–44* https://doi.org/10.1177/1477878509104318.

Perry, W. G. (1999). *Forms of ethical and intellectual development in the college years*. Jossey-Bass.

Retrieval Practice [Website]. Retrieved from https://www.retrievalpractice.org/retrievalpractice.

Roksa, J., Silver, B. R., Deutschlander, D., & Whitley, S. E. (2020). Navigating the first year of college: Siblings, parents, and first-generation students' experiences. *Sociological Forum, 35*(3), 565–86. doi:10.1111/socf.12617.

Rosenthal, R., & Jacobson, L. (1968). Pygmalion in the classroom. *The Urban Review, 3*, 16–20. https://doi.org/10.1007/BF02322211.

Ryan, R. M., & Deci, E. L. (2000). Self-determination theory and the facilitation of intrinsic motivation, social development, and well-being. *American Psychologist, 55*(1), 68–78. https://doi.org/10.1037/0003-066X.55.1.68.

Ryan, R. M., & Deci, E. L. (2006). Self☐regulation and the problem of human autonomy: Does psychology need choice, self-determination, and will? *Journal of Personality, 74*(6), 1557–86.

Schunk, D. H., & DiBenedetto, M. K. (2020). Motivation and social cognitive theory. *Contemporary Educational Psychology*, 60, Article 101832. doi:10.1016/j.cedpsych.2019.101832.

Schunk, D. H., & Usher, E. L. (2019). Social cognitive theory and motivation. In R. M. Ryan (Ed.), *The Oxford handbook of human motivation* (2nd ed., pp. 11–26). Oxford University Press.

Schunk, D. H., & Zimmerman, B. J. (Eds.). (2008). *Motivation and self-regulated learning: Theory, research, and applications.* Lawrence Erlbaum.

Shapiro, J. R. (2011). Different groups, different threats: A multi-threat approach to the experience of stereotype threats. *Personality and Social Psychology Bulletin, 37*(4), 464–80. https://doi.org/10.1177/0146167211398140

Skinner, B. F. (1976). *About behaviorism*. Vintage Books.

Steele, C. M., & Aronson, J. (1995). Stereotype threat and the intellectual test performance of African Americans. *Journal of Personality and Social Psychology, 69*(5), 797–811. https://doi.org/10.1037/0022-3514.69.5.797

Taylor, T., & Dibner, N. (2019). *Connect the dots: The collective power of relationships, memory and mindset in the classroom.* John Catt Bookshop.

Tenenbaum, H. R., & Ruck, M. D. (2007). Are teachers' expectations different for racial minority than for European American students? A meta-analysis. *Journal of Educational Psychology, 99*(2), 253–73.

van den Bergh, L., Denessen, E., Hornstra, L., Voeten, M., & Holland, R. W. (2010). The implicit prejudiced attitudes of teachers: Relations to teacher expectations and the ethnic achievement gap. *American Educational Research Journal, 47*(2), 497–527. https://doi.org/10.3102/0002831209353594.

Vroom, V. H. (1964). *Work and motivation*. Wiley.

Weiner, B. (2018). The legacy of an attribution approach to motivation and emotion: A no-crisis zone. *Motivation Science, 4*(1), 4–14. https://doi.org/10.1037/mot0000082.

Wigfield, A., & Eccles, J. S. (2000). Expectancy-value theory of achievement motivation. *Contemporary Educational Psychology, 25*, 68–81.

Yeager, D. S., Purdie-Vaughns, V., Garcia, J., Apfel, N., Brzustoski, P., Master, A., Hessert, W. T., Williams, M. E., & Cohen, G. L. (2014). Breaking the cycle of mistrust: Wise interventions to provide critical feedback across the racial divide.

Journal of Experimental Psychology: General, 143(2), 804–24. doi:10.1037/a0033906

Zee, M., & Koomen, M. Y. (2016). Teacher self-efficacy and its effects on classroom processes, student academic achievement, and teacher well-being: A synthesis of 40 years of research. *Review of Educational Research, 86,* 981–1015.

Zimmerman, B. J. (2000). Attaining self-regulation: A social cognitive perspective. In M. Boekaerts, P. R. Pintrich, & M. Zeidner (Eds.), Handbook of self-regulation (pp. 13–39). Academic Press.

Zimmerman, B. J., & Moylan, A. R. (2009). Self-regulation: Where metacognition and motivation intersect. In D. J. Hacker, J. Dunlosky, & A. C. Graesser (Eds.), *Handbook of metacognition in education* (pp. 299–315). Routledge/Taylor & Francis Group.

Zlate, S., & Cucui, G. (2015). Motivation and performance in higher education. *Procedia—Social and Behavioral Sciences, 180,* 468–76.

Fostering Relationships, Engagement, and Community to Enhance Classroom Management

Eve Dieringer, Michael Ferretti, and Kathleen Neagle Sokolowski

This chapter will present ideas and suggestions for classroom management in terms of fostering connections with the students and building engagement and community in the classroom through the lenses of a third-grade teacher, a district administrator, and a college professor. From the elementary teacher perspective, the teacher, the underpinning of a student's education, must hear every child's voice; acknowledge the paramount import of relationships; design lessons that support academic, social, and emotional growth; and initiate a strong link with the home.

From the administrator perspective, district-wide policies should be grounded in procedures that cultivate constructive relationships, where teachers meet their students at the door, talking about the recent sports event or drama club activity. In this way, restorative practice might replace punitive disciplinary measures.

From the higher education perspective, now more than ever, teacher preparation programs must fast-track their efforts to increase diversity; students need to see teachers who look like them and share cultural, ethnic, and racial similarities. Teacher candidates must meet the demands of engagement and recognize the cultural and linguistic background of their students as they navigate the requirements of certification.

Teachers play the most critical role in student achievement (Marzano, 2003), but considering them strictly as classroom managers (similar to being in business setting) would not account for many factors that need to be considered in teaching. Students are complex; managing is not enough. The teacher must cultivate relationships and simultaneously engage all students. The teacher, above all, is responsible for the learning achievement of all students.

Marzano's (2003) research, along with Wright et al.'s (1997), provides a foundation upon which to build an understanding of the need for an effective—hopefully a highly effective—educator. These esteemed researchers, however, do not detail the ingredients for an effective teacher. They do not supply a magic formula, recipe, prescription, or blueprint for the educators to guarantee that all students will flourish.

How do we train and ensure that every classroom comes outfitted with this "classroom manager?" The roots must begin in the teacher preparation college and university classrooms, through rigorous demands of teacher certification and field experiences. The higher education classrooms, in concert with supportive, inspiring cooperating teachers and clinical supervisors, furnish the foundation.

WHAT IS CLASSROOM MANAGEMENT?

"Classroom management consists of the practices and procedures a teacher uses to maintain the environment in which instruction and learning can take place" (Wong et al., 2018, p. 5). Wong et al.'s model of classroom management, focused on establishing sound classroom procedures, has been plausible for decades. However, education has changed dramatically, and what we have learned over time is that the most effective classroom managers build strong relationships with students and establish procedures that ensure a safe and engaging learning environment.

What we continue to learn is that the safest and most well-managed classrooms are those where the teachers have created communities in their classrooms and where students are given voice in the classroom. These effective classroom managers have also introduced the importance of being culturally responsive and managing students under the guise of acknowledging the diversity of students and the specific needs that are required to manage such a diverse population.

Culturally responsive management is as much an art form as it is a research-based theory. A teacher who can manage students effectively focuses on many teaching components, especially appropriate curriculum that is delivered with fidelity, and effective communication that recognizes the emotional, social, ethnic, cultural, and cognitive needs of students. Effectively managing students generally involves the ability to develop a classroom social environment in which students cooperate with one another and their teacher while making connections to what is being taught (Brown, 2004).

Stereotypes and Perceptions

It is imperative to dismiss the notion that there are "bad" students. The classroom management conversation should never be connected to the words "discipline," "bad student," and/or "punishment." Effective classroom management at any educational level is about establishing procedures and building sound relationships that enable students to feel safe while learning (Curwin, Mendler, & Mendler, 2008). Once educators realize their role is to make students more productive members of their learning community, the quicker the process is to more effective classroom management techniques and the less use of punishment for poor behavior or a failure to follow procedures.

Educators should never lose sight of the fact that they are working with children and that children will always make mistakes as they work through the difficulties faced at home and in school. Students who struggle with procedures should never be stereotyped as "bad" students, nor should they be marked as troublemakers. The causes of poor behavior are sometimes linked to outside influences and distractors in students' lives that lead them to act inappropriately in school. Some students start their school day with anxiety because of a difficult morning, only to lash out in school because they are returning to the dysfunction when school ends.

Who could have guessed that so many students would be victimized by violence and bullying, some rationally fearing for their lives? It is equally doubtful that most teachers would have thought that nearly every class would be filled with a group of students of wide-ranging intellectual, cultural, and emotional diversity. Now part of the fabric of education, inclusion is here to stay (Curwin et al., 2008, p. 2).

The changes in our student body have forced educators to be more flexible and responsive when managing a classroom. COVID-19 has challenged all—students and teachers at all levels, from prekindergarten through doctoral programs. The switch to fully online learning called for new methods of instruction and new ways to keep students engaged. As the classroom instruction in many instances will continue in at least a hybrid format, in the future, new issues will be sure to face students and, more importantly, new methods of classroom management. When a teacher buys into being a culturally responsive classroom manager, the shift in thinking should include "a focus on equity, inclusion and cultural responsiveness so that the techniques will be more effective in promoting academic and behavioral functioning for students of color, and in turn, reduce disproportionality" (Gaias et al., 2019, p. 125). This is especially important as the student population increases in diversity at a pace that requires educators to give it equal focus when planning instruction and planning a management system.

Building Relationships

To be effective relationship builders, educators must take a personal and vested interest in their students. Effective teaching is about making the day's lesson relate to everyone in the classroom. The ability to teach at this level has become more challenging because of the diversity in education as well as the need to teach and be cognizant of the social, emotional, and academic needs of children. The teachers who find ways to build relationships and show vested interest in their students' lives have found success. All students value their teacher's attention.

Teachers can enhance the relationship with students in the classroom. Some teacher actions can include the following:

a. Meeting and greeting every student individually as they enter the classroom;
b. Engaging in informal conversations with students about their interests before, during, and after class;
c. Greeting students outside of the classroom settings; and
d. Being aware and complimenting students for their accomplishments and important events in their lives (Marzano & Marzano, 2003).

All of Marzano's suggestions are page one of any text that speaks to building relationships as a key component to effective classroom management. Again, there is no mention of discipline or consequences as a result of a failure to follow procedures. Once the teacher has established a relationship built upon trust and genuine interest, there will not be a need for formal discipline; rather, there can be a constructive dialogue that maintains a student's dignity and maintains a teacher's control of situations.

Encouraging Engagement

To learn and achieve, students must be engaged. Engagement is an integral element of the relationship. The first grader, listening transfixed on a rug as her teacher reads *The Day You Begin* by Jacqueline Woodson (2018), the sixth grader captivated by discussions of *The Hate U Give* by Angela Thomas (2017), and the tenth grader excitedly researching her culture to share with classmates are absorbed and engaged in their learning. Ralph Fletcher (2013) advises elementary teachers to encourage young male writers to be actively engaged in the process of writing. His advice is clear: "Worry about their engagement first; the quality will come later" (para 1).

Texts, lectures, documentaries, and class presentations alone cannot prepare teacher candidates for the challenges ahead. In addition, the candidates require authentic experiences in the field to translate the research and coursework into action. Literacy strategies must be communicated from Calkins, Beers, Keene and Zimmerman, Fountas, and Pinnell to all students: gifted, struggling, special needs, English-language learners. One teacher preparation program in suburban New York began placing all teacher candidates for their first field experience in high-needs schools with diverse student bodies.

For example, the elementary candidates spent two hours each week for one semester in a school with 386 elementary students in the 2018–2019 academic year. The students' ethnicity is documented as follows: 84.2 percent Hispanic or Latino, 13.7 percent Black or African American, and 1.6 percent White (New York State Education Department, 2019a).

The teachers, while not exactly reflecting the makeup of the student population, were more diverse than most schools in this suburban region. At this elementary school, with a total of twenty-four teachers, eight are identified as African American (33.3%), seven Hispanic or Latino (29.2%), eight White (33.3%), and one Asian (Diamond, 2019).

The necessity for this experience was underscored during a discussion with three students who were completing their required observations. One openly admitted, "I expected chaos because it was a high-needs school" (C. Schecht, personal communication, November 26, 2019). Her own educational background was not at all similar to the demographic composition she experienced while observing.

She found, however, that the teacher was "very approachable" and the students were respectful and eager to ask questions. The same student said the teacher mentioned that many parents were not involved. Rather than accepting the teacher's solution, the candidate must learn, throughout the preparation program, to question "Why?" and "What can I do to ensure an inclusive environment when I have my own classroom?"

Another commented that this was "an eye-opening experience that makes you go out of your comfort zone" (R. DiLorenzo, personal communication, November 26, 2019). The third student noted that the New York State Culturally Responsive-Sustaining Education Framework was introduced at a board of education meeting. She questioned, "What were they doing before?" yet acknowledged, "But it gives a sense of awareness" (J. Contrejas, personal communication, November 26, 2019).

Will a mere thirty hours in one semester prepare teacher candidates to be effective practitioners? Will their additional field experiences afford them exceptional role models and opportunities to observe and emulate professionals who have developed relationships and engaged all students? It is incumbent on the colleges and universities to guarantee the academic foundation and field experiences that guarantee all students the groundwork for a productive life and career.

Cultural and linguistic similarities between student and teacher, the perfectly planned lesson, and the passion for the content are inadequate without the relationship. Relationships are at the very core of student achievement. When interviewed for the teacher preparation program, the candidates' responses invariably pointed to that one teacher "who cared about me, who knew me as a person" (M. O'Callaghan, personal communication, November 13, 2019). In his classic, *Letters to a Young Teacher*, Jonathan Kozol (2007) explained the importance of establishing relationships to "Francesca." In his first teaching position in an impoverished Boston neighborhood, Kozol simply promised, "I told them I was there to stay" (p. 10).

The Harvard Teaching Fellow program cites "relationship building" in its concise mission statement, alongside "academic rigor" and "continuous learning" (Harvard Graduate School of Education, 2020). Edverette Brewster, a student in the teaching and learning program, commented, "But any teacher—no matter the race or age—you have to build relationships and get to know your students" (Moss, 2016, para 16).

BUILDING A CLASSROOM COMMUNITY OF LEARNERS

There are so many aspects of education that are beyond a teacher's control. While teachers have many choices taken out of their hands, perhaps the most important choice is to "humanize and not dehumanize a child," as Ginott (1972, p. 13) said, and this is definitely the choice of teachers. Their words, actions, and intentions critically matter in building and maintaining a positive classroom community.

Despite the mandated curriculum, the size of the class, the schedule of push ins and pullouts, and the standardized tests, there is so much that a teacher can influence: the way a student is greeted each day, what is emphasized about making mistakes and taking risks, how we treat each other, and living together as a community of learners. The teacher has tremendous impact in creating the classroom climate.

How can teachers establish a classroom community of learners where everyone has a voice, feels safe to make mistakes, is respected, and teaching and learning seamlessly occur throughout the day? How can we create this type of environment despite the challenges of teaching students from trauma, students who come from poverty, cultural differences among students, and differences in abilities (i.e., physical, emotional, and intellectual)?

Teacher Beliefs and Mindset

The first step for a teacher in establishing a safe and equitable classroom community is to believe that all students are learners who are capable of meeting high standards through flexible strategies, differentiated instruction, and different entry points. How a teacher views her students is critical. Does she form ideas about them based on their culture, race, gender, religion, or socioeconomic status? Are expectations high for all students? According to American Psychological Association's (2015) "Top 20 Principles from Psychology for pre-K to 12 Teaching and Learning," teachers' expectations have an impact on "students' opportunities to learn, their motivation and their learning outcomes" (p. 19).

Teacher expectations can be tied to the concept known as the *Pygmalion effect* or *self-fulfilling prophesy*. First introduced by Rosenthal and Jacobson (1968), the Pygmalion effect is the idea that expectations of something to occur can in fact make it happen, and as a self-fulfilling prophecy, it is a belief that becomes a positive reality. For example, if students question their ability due to lack of encouragement from the teacher, students begin believing it, and while they might not have failed otherwise, because they stop studying, they fail and make the prophecy true.

Workman (2012), in her article on teacher expectations and self-fulfilling prophesy, also illustrated another example:

> A teacher might set lower standards for historically low-achieving students or he/she might perceive various students' behaviors differently. A delayed response from a non- minority, more affluent student might be perceived as thoughtful consideration, while the same delayed response from a minority, lower-income student might be considered as a lack of understanding. These differences in teacher behavior convey expectations to students, which can significantly affect their own behavior in ways that impede academic achievement. (p. 2)

When teachers communicate faulty expectations to students, the students may then begin to act in a fashion that leads to the confirmation of the teachers' original expectations. Therefore, it is important for educators to be self-aware and unpack their own biases. Ahmed (2018) challenged teachers to look at how they use language in the classroom and how it positions students. Do they use language that is a negative judgment in describing student behavior such as "disruptive" or "tantrums," or do they focus more on the actual descriptions of behavior without a negative connotation (e.g., a student carries a soccer ball)?

Ahmed (2018) also asserted, "Language keeps us at the center of what we believe is expected and therefore socially acceptable . . . But we don't have license to certify normal. That is a basic tenet in the work of social comprehension. While diversity is the word of the day, when we decenter the dominant, normative narratives in society, we make way for not only diversity, but also inclusion" (p. xxix). Teachers need to believe all their students are capable of learning and achieving excellence, and are deserving of a quality education. By unpacking their own biases and maintaining high standards for all students, the teachers can allow all students to feel welcome and included.

Having high and equitable expectations for all students is key, as is believing in a growth mindset. Dr. Carol Dweck (2016) described fixed mindsets and growth mindsets in her book *Mindset: The New Psychology of Success*. A teacher with a fixed mindset might label students as "capable" and "not capable" and teach them according to that belief, communicating to some students that they cannot meet the standards. An educator with a growth mindset understands that abilities are fluid and can be placed on a continuum, where they can be further developed through instruction, effort, and practice.

Teachers can model a growth mindset by sharing profiles of high-achieving people who discuss their failures along the way to being successful. Teachers can demonstrate resilience and making mistakes when learning something new. The expectation that "We are all learning" and "Mistakes are part of the process" can help students realize they have the power to develop their skills and abilities. Every student deserves to be part of a classroom where the teacher values the whole person and believes in the student's ability to achieve great things.

Strategies to Build a Community of Learners

Teachers can build a welcoming learning community from the first day of school. Learning students' names and pronouncing their names correctly is a way teachers show students respect. Allowing space for students to share their interests and passions is a way that teachers can begin to get to know each child. Some teachers ask students to bring in a collection of items that represent themselves and share this with the class. Taking a few minutes each day to have a few students talk about their collection helps them to get to know one another and sets up the expectation that each person is important and worth getting to know. This helps students to see the similarities between themselves while also holding space for the differences.

Beginning each day with a morning meeting is a routine that builds community throughout the year. Students greet one another by name each day and might participate in a short icebreaker activity, an academic game, or a math number sense routine. Assigning jobs to students also helps build a collaborative culture and lets students have a role in how the classroom runs.

The texts a teacher chooses to share with a classroom of students can have a powerful impact, both academically and socioemotionally. Rudine Sims Bishop (1990), professor emerita of education at Ohio State University, drew the following analogy:

> Books are sometimes windows, offering views of worlds that may be real or imagined, familiar or strange. These windows are also sliding glass doors, and readers have only to walk through in imagination to become part of whatever world has been created or recreated by the author. (p. ix)

The current emphasis on equity and diversity is also influencing choices teachers make in the selection of texts to highlight voices of Blacks, Native Americans, or authors with disabilities.

Sharing a wide range of books with students helps them to expand their worldviews and develop empathy for people who might be different from them. By reading aloud books where the main characters are from diverse cultures, differently abled, part of nontraditional family structures, and living in places foreign to the students who are listening, teachers decenter the "norm" and allow students to widen their worldview.

Classroom conversations about the themes and characters can strengthen the community of learners around these stories and the universal struggles we all face. In addition to reading aloud, the teacher should have a plentiful and diverse classroom library and allow students to self-select books to read and enjoy. The books shared send a message as to who and what is valued. As educators, we need to make the community as inclusive and welcoming as possible.

Fostering Partnerships with Families

In striving to make the classroom a community for students, educators must acknowledge that students each belong to a family, though not all families are structured the same. As educators, it is important to reach out to all families and include them in their child's school experience. Teachers can do this in a myriad of ways.

Some educators share their class happenings via social media sites like Facebook, Twitter, and Instagram to help flatten the walls of the classroom and allow families an insider's look at the learning that happens each day. Other educators create a class website or blog to share information with families.

Positive notes home and phone calls take time but are worth the investment in building a positive relationship between the teacher, the child, and the family. Family dialogue journals are another way to include families and caregivers in their child's education. A teacher poses a question in writing, a child answers, and a family member writes back, adding one's own response as well. This three-way conversation can open the door to more honest communication and a stronger sense of community.

Figure 3.1 Family journal entry from the Alcruz family.

For example, during the 2020–2021 school year, figure 3.1 presents a family dialogue journal reflecting a child's response to the following question: Show me how you feel when you are doing remote learning. In this example, the kindergartner experienced initial difficulties with online learning during the pandemic, but due to virtual and family journal exchanges with the teacher and the parents, the child was able to overcome the behavioral challenges.

When a teacher communicates with families, it is important to genuinely share what the teacher appreciates and likes about the student before discussing any misconduct or concerns. When family members feel that the teacher cares about their child, it is much easier to hear about a child's actions that might need correcting. Families and educators can work together to be on the same team, always supporting a student's growth and achievement.

RESTORATIVE PRACTICES IN EDUCATION

What Are Restorative Practices?

Restorative practices involve processes that aim to prevent and counteract conflicts and wrongdoing by actively engaging participants, by forming relationships, and building a sense of community (Wachtel, 2013). Furthermore, Smith et al. (2015) described, "The restorative practices movement is an offshoot of the restorative justice model used by courts and law enforcement agencies. In this model, mutually consenting victims and offenders meet so the victim has a voice, and the offender can make amends and show remorse" (p. 4).

The use of restorative practices in the classroom is part of this transformation from punitive forms of discipline to proactive measures of building open dialogue to create a sense of community within classrooms. The relationship between effective classroom management and the use of restorative practices in the classroom derives from the realization that the more punitive, discipline model used in most classrooms has become antiquated and ineffective, while the restorative model provides opportunities to strengthen the relationships between and among teachers and students and encourages everyone to have a voice in the classroom.

Five goals of restorative practices in the classroom include the following:

a. Addressing and discussing the needs of the school community;
b. Building healthy relationships between and among students and educators;
c. Resolving conflicts, holding individuals and groups accountable;

d. Repairing harm and restoring positive relationships; and
e. Preventing, reducing, and improving harmful behavior (Schott Foundation, 2014).

According to Costello and colleagues (as cited in Wachtel & McCold, 2004), the basic premise behind restorative practice is "that human beings are happiest, healthiest and most likely to make positive changes in their behavior when those in positions of authority do things WITH them rather than TO them or FOR them" (p. 94). This concept is about the equity that restorative practice adheres to in its definition and in its implementation. It is about the idea that human relationships are best when there is free expression of dialogue and emotion and that there are safe processes for students to respond to conflict. The process also teaches students to be self-aware and to trust in the system so that whichever side of the table they sit at (victim or offender), they will be heard and be offered an opportunity to make amends.

The social discipline window is a graphic that illustrates this premise and shows how restorative practices differ from other modes of discipline. The social discipline window (see figure 3.2) describes four basic approaches to maintaining social norms and behavioral boundaries. The four are

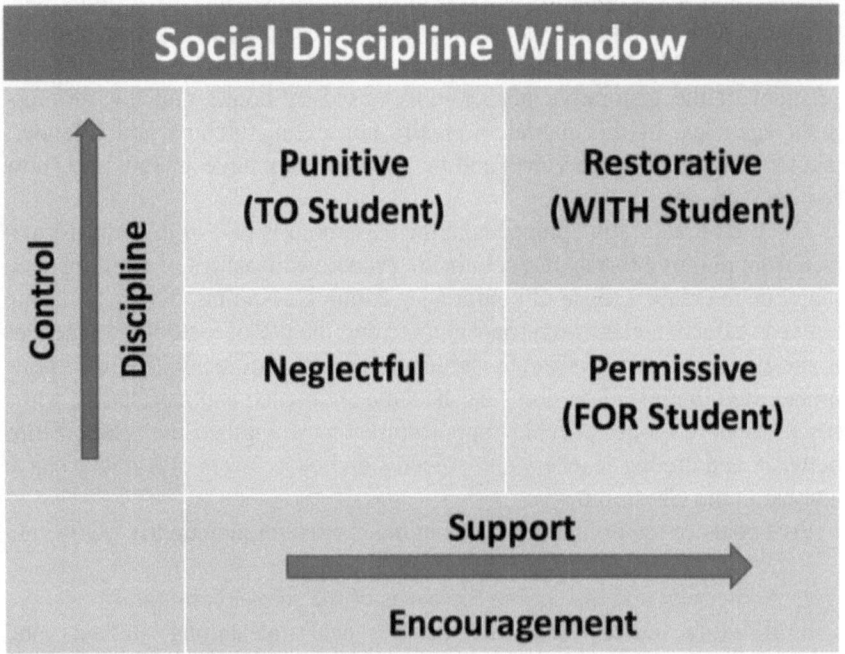

Figure 3.2 The social discipline window.
Source: Adapted from Wachtel (2005).

represented as different combinations of high or low control and high or low support. The restorative domain combines both high control and high support and is characterized by doing things with people, rather than to them or for them (Wachtel, 2005).

Why Might Restorative Practices Be Implemented in Classrooms?

Restorative Circles are strategies borrowed from restorative practices and applied in classrooms to develop relationships, build communities, and respond to conflicts and problems that arise. As an equitable measure, it gives everyone an opportunity to speak and be heard. Nicole Lavonne Smith (2020), a restorative justice practitioner, explains very well the origins of this practice:

> Restorative justice circles are born out of indigenous (pre-colonized) societies around the world. Circles tap into our communal nature, and our desire to be in a positive relationships with one another. In circles, no one is seen as dispensable and everyone is valued for their knowledge and unique gifts. In this way, communities remain whole and reciprocal. Circles build accountability between individuals and the larger community. (para 2)

The importance and benefits of the circles can be connected to the following dimensions:

- **Equality:** Literally everyone in the circle has an equal seating.
- **Safety and Trust:** You can see everyone in the circle, so nothing is hidden.
- **Responsibility:** Everyone has a chance to play a role in the outcome of the circle.
- **Facilitation**: The circle reminds the leader to facilitate rather than lecture.
- **Ownership**: Collectively, the participants feel the circle is theirs.
- **Connections**: These connections are built as everyone listens to everyone else's responses. (Costello et al., 2019, p. 22)

How Can Restorative Practices Be Implemented in Classrooms?

Educators should have a list of procedures that they want followed in their classroom. The word *procedure* was chosen specifically because the use of the word *rule* usually connects to the word *punishment*. Establishing effective classroom procedures sets expectations for students and speaks to a collaborative effort that the students should participate in creating. Establishing expectations and equitable procedures also strengthens the students' understanding of a moral code in the classroom or a set of unwritten values that the teacher implements into the procedures. This is another way to live up to the mantra that an educator's role is to assist students in being more productive members of their community. If teachers truly want their students to be more productive, it is imperative that they teach their students how to become more effective communicators.

Teachers cannot simply rely on the dialogue that is predicated by the day's lesson or the interactions that are routine in a classroom setting. Currently, there is a very effective and newly innovative method through which teachers and students communicate as a group, giving students a real voice in the classroom community: the use of circles.

The use of Restorative Circles as an effective communication and community-building tool has proven to be an effective way for teachers to build relationships and address conflict within the classroom community. These circles create safe spaces for students and help to build connections within the classroom community. The circle space becomes a forum for accountability and communication (Bintliff, 2014).

Restorative Circles are used effectively in the classroom for a variety of reasons. These circles have specific formats and purposes. Some circle formats include the Basic Circle, the Popcorn Circle, and the Fishbowl Circle. Specific circle formats have evolved to address and support specific situations, because these circle formats utilize specific procedural strategies to facilitate the circle discussion. There are also specific reasons why circles are convened in the classroom.

Responsive Circles are an effective way to deal with classroom issues in the moment. They can be effective for discussing and solving class problems. Preparation and presentation prior to the convocation of any circle are vital to success. The Responsive Circle can be facilitated using either a sequential structure (e.g., discussion moves clockwise around the circle) or a nonsequential structure (e.g., random order of participation). The use of the circle and the plan to discuss the conflict/problem within the circle is what creates the open forum of communication within the classroom community (Costello et al., 2019).

To plan for the implementation of an effective Responsive Circle to address a classroom issue, there are three target areas of focus for any Responsive Circle to discuss:

- Think about what was happening in the class that wasn't working and have people take responsibility for what they were doing to contribute to the issue.
- Ask what kind of atmosphere students and teachers ideally want in the classroom.

Fishbowl Circle

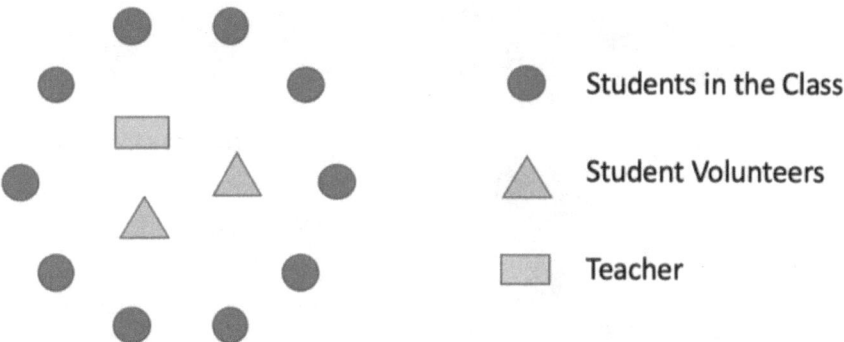

Figure 3.3 Fishbowl Circle.

- Reflect and think about what each person is going to do to help attain that ideal (Costello et al. 2019, p. 57).

The Fishbowl Circle is another example of an effective Restorative Circle. A Fishbowl Circle (see figure 3.3) can be especially effective when used to build skills or when discussing sensitive or important topics that require careful listening (Smith et al., 2015). The students in the inner circle discuss the topic at hand while the students in the outer circle observe and take notes. Outer circle students are invited to join the inner circle if they want to participate in the dialogue. The circles are a positive method to build classroom norms and for instilling values within the classroom community. Again, the Fishbowl Circle may use either a sequential or nonsequential structure.

A sequential circle has a fixed order for student participation (see figure 3.4). This type of circle is especially effective with students who would normally sit quietly and observe the group. This circle can be used as a response to an incident, a change or establishment of procedures, or for conflict resolution. In this scenario, the teacher serves as a facilitator and offers a "talking piece," which is an item that will serve as a visual reminder of who is speaking. The talking piece is passed around and students take turns participating (Smith et al., 2015).

This structure allows for open dialogue, student participation and interaction, and the building of relationships and classroom community. The sequential circle elicits student "voice" in the classroom community. A sequential circle uses a structured dialogue that elicits open dialogue to build relationships and deal with conflict in the classroom community. The more the teacher can facilitate proactive dialogue, the more the students will buy

Sequential Restorative Circle

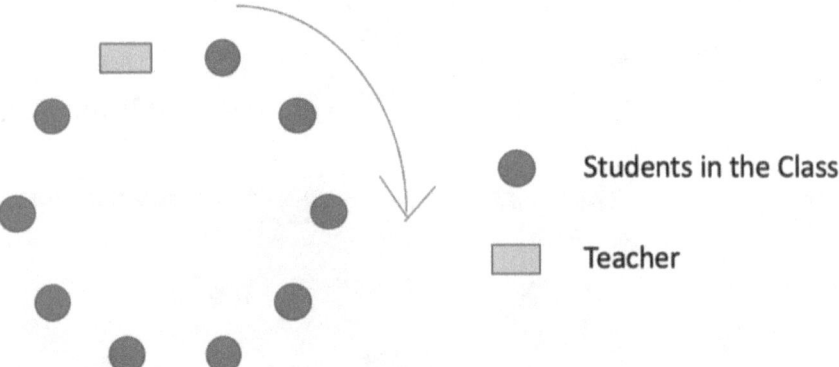

Figure 3.4 Sequential Restorative Circle.

into the procedures and the moral value the teacher is trying to establish in the classroom community.

A proactive circle is used for meaningful discussions in groups within the classroom community (Gregory et al., 2016). In the sequential circle process, the teacher is the true facilitator of information and dialogue, and the students become equal voices in the discussion group. As Costello et al. (2019) advised, "When issues arise, lean on the social capital that has been built using circles. Problems then become opportunities, and the classroom becomes a functioning unit" (p. 49). Once a routine is established, the students will be able to create their own circles and invite their teacher to observe or act as a liaison to further discussion.

A nonsequential circle does not have a fixed order of participation and allows for open dialogue when students want to respond to one another as often as they choose (Smith et al., 2015). It is important for the teacher to serve as facilitator to keep the discussion organized and focused on the topic. It is also important for the teacher to remind the students that everyone is welcome to participate and that every opinion is vital to the potential reparation of the problem. Preparedness and a precursor discussion will always assist in an active and successful nonsequential circle.

The additional kinds of circles based on the restorative justice approach are explained in table 3.1.

Table 3.1. Types of Restorative Circles.

Type of Restorative Circle	Purpose	Application
Basic Connection Circle or Check-in Circle	To provide opportunities for all students to check in at the beginning of discussion	• Encourages all circle participants to engage in the discussion process • May use both sequential and non-sequential structure • Only in a Basic Circle format
Response Circle	To discuss and/or problem-solve issues	• Students name the issue or problem • Students contribute ideas for solutions • May use both sequential and non-sequential structure • May be in a Basic, Popcorn, Fishbowl, or Spiral Circle format
Story of the Day Circle	To discuss special events or unusual experiences	Enhances learning: • To create story lines with plot • To elaborate with details • To discover an appreciation for life-enriching experiences • May use both sequential and non-sequential structure • May be in a Basic, Popcorn, Fishbowl, or Spiral Circle format
Something Special Circle	To learn about individual students and their interests	• Used to learn more about individual students • Used to learn about shared interests • Used to build classroom community

What Are the Long-Term Impacts of Restorative Practices in the Classroom?

Graham (2017) explained, "When students understand and subscribe to the norms and values of their classrooms or schools, they are much better able to act in accordance with those values, even in the absence of adult supervision. Furthermore, students whose experiences in school have supported their development of a sense of self-efficacy are better able to share responsibility for creating a positive and supportive environment" (p. 507). Once the community is established, management becomes a self-sufficient process in which the students take ownership.

It is imperative that students feel empowered and believe they have a voice in the classroom for this process to be effective. The use of circles in the classroom is the first step in building the restorative practice model and will be the most useful platform to effectively communicate, resolve conflict, and build trust.

ADDRESSING INSTITUTIONAL NEEDS TO FOSTER RELATIONSHIPS, ENGAGEMENT, AND COMMUNITY

Rarely does the cultural and racial makeup of the teacher mirror that of the students. School districts across the country have introduced initiatives to increase diversity among the teaching force (Carver-Thomas, 2018). The U.S. Department of Education Schools and Staffing Survey specifies that 82 percent of the public school teaching force labeled themselves as White (U.S. Department of Education, 2016, p. 1). These numbers do not correspond to the public school student population. In 2012, White students numbered 51 percent. By 2024, it is projected that White students will number 46 percent, Hispanic students 29 percent, and Black students 15 percent (U.S. Department of Education, 2016, p. 5).

Research consistently discloses positive outcomes when students are assigned to a teacher with the same race/ethnicity (Ordway, 2017). For example, a North Carolina study found that with same-race teachers, the rate of Black students' expulsion, as well as in- and out-of-school suspensions, decreased. This reduction applied to males and females, and elementary, middle, and high school levels, regardless of free and reduced lunch parameters (Lindsay & Hart, 2017).

Cherng and Halpin (2016) supported the argument for minority recruitment, finding that minority students' perceptions of minority teachers were more favorable compared to perceptions of White teachers. The authors concluded that minority teachers can empower not only minority but all students, as they are more likely equipped to form strong connections with them.

Egalite et al. (2015) determined that significant positive effects, although small, were found when students were assigned to teachers of the same race. These gains were found in reading and mathematics from grades three through ten. Their study also found that Black and White students who previously were classified as low performing especially benefit from a teacher whose race was the same.

When Black students are matched with a Black teacher, studies indicated an increase in achievement alongside social and emotional gains. "The benefit of having a Black teacher for just 1 year in elementary school can persist over several years, especially for Black students from low-income families"

(Carver-Thomas, 2018, p. 4). However, it is not only the Black students who profit but non-Black students as well.

The Harvard Teaching Fellow program, registering their first cohort of students in the spring of 2016, sought out a diverse group of students. Recruiter and lecturer Sarah Leibel noted, "It's really important that students have people who reflect back to them their language, their culture, their ethnicity, their religion" (Moss, 2016). This master teacher added the students' need for "mirrors and windows" in literature: "And we know that in the teaching profession, there really are not enough mirrors" (Moss, 2016).

Ta-Nehesi Coates (2015) documented his excitement about learning Black history and literature as a student at Howard University. Geneva Gay (2000) retold the story of two siblings who scored highly on tests and excitedly discussed Mildred Taylor's (1976) *Roll of Thunder, Hear My Cry*. While these two students should have excelled throughout their school careers, they did not. They achieved when the author was African American; they achieved when there were "mirrors and windows."

Situations abound in scholarly research that denote the teacher who misunderstands the student. Researchers recount the story of an African American student whose teacher (also African American but schooled in primarily White communities) demanded quiet passivity, unlike the expectations in his home (Weinstein et al., 2003, p. 269).

A second grader from Vietnam answered, "Yes," when her teacher asks if she understood the assignment. The seven-year-old's work indicated she did not, and her teacher was irritated. The translation for "yes" is not precise. These cultural misperceptions are often followed by a reprimand, a negative report card comment, or punitive action.

The role of the teacher as "classroom manager" is crucial, as highlighted by Marzano and Marzano (2003, p. 1). In a classroom with no parameters for behavior, little teaching and learning can ensue. Neither teacher nor student thrives. Wright et al. (1997) supported this thesis. In their study of 60,000 elementary-aged students, the authors argued that "*effective teachers appear to be effective with students of all achievement levels regardless of the levels of heterogeneity in their classes*" (p. 63) (emphasis in original).

Haycock's (1998) research validates the argument. A student placed in the class of a highly effective teacher may gain 52 percentile points within one year in contrast to the student in the class of the least effective teacher, whose growth is approximately 14 percentile points. The difference between student achievement in the effective "manager's" classroom compared to the ineffective teacher's classroom is quite evident.

In his meta-analysis, Marzano (2003) reiterated that the most significant influence on student achievement is the teacher. His research, with comparable inferences, concentrated on the average school and average teacher, the least effective school and least effective teacher, the most effective school and the most effective teacher, and finally, the least effective school and the most effective teacher. The cumulative effects, over a three-year span, on achievement between students with the least effective teacher compared to the most effective teacher, are astounding. The student with the most effective teacher gained 83 percentile points while the student with the least effective teacher demonstrated a 29 percentile gain (Marzano, 2003).

HIGHER EDUCATION PERSPECTIVE

From the perspective of current teacher preparation programs, there is a critical need to seek and recruit a more diverse body of future educators. In addition, teacher education programs should require a more comprehensive and sequential approach to meet cultural, ethnic, racial, and linguistic needs within the curriculum and practice. Teacher candidates must meet the demands of engagement with diverse student populations and represent competency in addressing the needs of their specific students.

Nine hundred fifteen teacher preparation programs in forty-one states and the District of Columbia participate in the edTPA (n.d.), which is a performance-based assessment of teacher candidates to determine their subject-specific knowledge and skill readiness to teach in classroom settings. The initiative was developed by Stanford University and the Stanford Center for Assessment, Learning and Equity (SCALE, 2018) and guided by the American Association of Colleges for Teacher Education (AACTE). This portfolio-based assessment focuses on these three areas: planning, instruction, and the assessment of student learning.

To ensure that the teacher candidates understand that engagement with students is critical, the edTPA devotes three of eighteen rubrics to student engagement (SCALE, 2018). Rubric 6, the Learning Environment, asks the elementary teacher candidate, "How does the candidate demonstrate a positive literacy learning environment that supports students' engagement in learning?" (SCALE, 2018, p. 19). Rubric 7, Engaging Students in Learning, asks, "How does the candidate actively engage students in integrating strategies and skills to comprehend OR compose text?" (SCALE, 2018, p. 22).

In the mathematics portion, the candidate is asked to design a "re-engagement lesson to further student learning" (SCALE, 2018, p. 50). The secondary candidates also address student engagement in the learning environment in two of the eighteen rubrics.

In the edTPA glossary, *cultural* is defined as follows: "Refers to the cultural backgrounds and practices that students bring to the learning environment, such as traditions, languages and dialects, worldviews, literature, art, and so on, that a teacher can draw upon to support learning" (p. 46). To guarantee student engagement, the teacher must consider the students' cultural background as well as their academic strengths and limitations.

The edTPA probes, "What do you know about your students' everyday experiences, cultural and language backgrounds and practices, and interests?" (SCALE, 2019, p. 11). While planning the lesson for this portfolio requirement, teacher candidates must attend to their students' "social, cultural, or community assets" (SCALE, 2019, p. 15). It is not surprising that engaging students and having an in-depth awareness of students' cultures are linked in Rubric 7 (SCALE, 2019, p. 23). For example, it is not sufficient to celebrate Black History Month and acknowledge the single day of Eid al-Fitr with a day off from school.

The New York State Education Department (2019b) has published the Culturally Responsive-Sustaining Education Framework in its sixty-three page document with four principles (p. 7):

- Welcoming and Affirming Environment
- High Expectations and Rigorous Instruction
- Inclusive Curriculum and Assessment
- Ongoing Professional Learning

Responsive strategies in peer-reviewed journals and academic texts, both past and present, advise teachers to acknowledge their own cultural biases (Weinstein et al., 2003) and create relationships with students (Deady, 2017; Marzano, 2003; New York University, Metropolitan Center for Urban Education, 2008).

CLOSING THOUGHTS

Teachers have the ability to create a positive mindset for learning for themselves and their students. The words and actions of teachers create a learning community where students know they belong and are safe to take risks when trying something new. Intentionally building relationships and making positive family connections can influence the type of community that will develop in a classroom.

Educators need not think of "managing" a classroom of students but instead working to foster a community where relationships matter and students are at the center of all the decisions made. The old model of clip charts and publicly showcasing a student's behavior is not aligned with the ideals of building relationships and understanding that making mistakes is how we learn. Rewards and punishments are not what motivate students in these classrooms; it is the intrinsic motivation of being part of an authentic learning community.

From the teacher perspective, educators must listen to students' voices, recognize the magnitude of relationships, create lessons that further not only academic but also social and emotional accomplishments, and ensure connections with the home.

From the administrator perspective, district-wide policies must promote positive relationships; in this regard, restorative practice might supplant punitive practices.

From the higher education perspective, teacher preparation programs must increase diversity; students need to see teachers who look like them and share cultural, ethnic, and racial similarities. As they traverse the demands of state certification, teacher candidates must understand the prerequisite of engagement for learning as well as recognize the cultural and linguistic backgrounds of their students. Engagement is fundamental.

REFERENCES

Ahmed, S. K. (2018). *Being the change: Lessons and strategies to teach social comprehension*. Heinemann.

American Psychological Association. (2015). *Top 20 principles from psychology for pre-K to 12 teaching and learning*. Retrieved from http:// www.apa.org/ed/schools/cpse/top-twenty-principles.pdf.

Bintliff, A. (2014, July 22). *Talking circles: For restorative justice and beyond.* Retrieved from https://www.learningforjustice.org/magazine/talking-circles-for-restorative-justice-and-beyond.

Bishop, R. S. (1990). Mirrors, windows and sliding glass doors. *Perspectives: Choosing and Using Books for the Classroom, 6*(3), ix–xi.

Brown, D. F. (2004). Urban teachers' professed classroom management strategies: Reflections of culturally responsive teaching. *Urban Education, 39*(3), 266–89. doi:10.1177/0042085904263258.

Carver-Thomas, D. (2018). *Diversifying the teaching profession: How to recruit and retain teachers of color.* Learning Policy Institute. Retrieved from https://learningpolicyinstitute.org/product/diversifying-teaching-profession-report.

Cherng, H. S., & Halpin P. F. (2016). The importance of minority teachers: Student perceptions of minority versus white teachers. *Educational Researcher, 45*(7), 407–20. https://journals.sagepub.com/doi/full/10.3102/0013189X16671718.

Coates, T. (2015). *Between the world and me* (1st ed.). Spiegel and Grau.

Costello, B., Wachtel, J., & Wachtel, T. (2019). *The restorative practices handbook for teachers, disciplinarians and administrators* (2nd ed.). International Institute for Restorative Practices.

Curwin, R. L., Mendler, A. N., & Mendler, B. D. (2008). *Discipline with dignity: New challenges, new solutions*. ASCD.

Dweck, C. S. (2016). *Mindset: Changing the way you think to fulfil your potential*. Ballantine Books.

edTPA (n.d.). *Participation map*. Retrieved from http://edtpa.aacte.org/state-policy.

Egalite, A. J., Kisida, B., & Winters, M. A. (2015, April). Representation in the classroom: The effect of own-race teachers on student achievement. *Economics of Education Review*, *45*, 44–52. https://doi.org/10.1016/j.econedurev.2015.01.007.

Fletcher, R. (2013, November). *Creating boy-friendly writing classrooms*. Retrieved from http://ralphfletcher.com/rf/wp-content/uploads/2013/11/Creating-Boy-Friendly-writing-classrooms.pdf.

Gaias, L. M., Johnson, S. L., Bottiani, J. H., Debnam, K. J., & Bradshaw, C. P. (2019). Examining teachers' classroom management profiles: Incorporating a focus on culturally responsive practice. *Journal of School Psychology*, *76*, 124–39. doi: 10.1016/j.jsp.2019.07.017.

Gay, G. (2000). *Culturally responsive teaching: Theory, research, and practice* (3rd ed.). Teachers College Press.

Ginott, H. (1972). *Teacher & child: A book for parents and teachers*. New York: Avon.

Graham, E. J. (2017). Authority or democracy? Integrating two perspectives on equitable classroom management in urban schools. *The Urban Review*, *50*(3), 493–515. doi: 10.1007/s11256-017-0443–8.

Gregory, A., Clawson, K., Davis, A., & Gerewitz, J. (2016). The promise of restorative practices to transform teacher-student relationships and achieve equity in school discipline. *Journal of Educational and Psychological Consultation*, *26*(4), 325–53. doi:10.1080/10474412.2014.929950.

Harvard Graduate School of Education. (2020). *About: Harvard teacher fellows*. Retrieved from https://htf.gse.harvard.edu/about.

Haycock, K. (1998). Good teaching matters . . . a lot. *Thinking K-16*, *3*(2), 1–14.

Kozol, J. (2007). *Letters to a young teacher*. Three Rivers Press.

Lindsay. C. A., & Hart, C. M. D. (2017). Exposure to same-race teachers and student disciplinary outcomes for black students in North Carolina. *Educational Evaluation and Policy Analysis*, *39*(3), 485–510. https://doi.org/10.3102/0162373717693109.

Marzano, R. J. (2003). *What works in schools: Translating research into action*. Association for Supervision and Curriculum Development.

Marzano, R. J., & Marzano, J. S. (2003). The key to classroom management. *Educational Leadership: Journal of the Department of Supervision and Curriculum Development*, *61*(1), 6–13.

Moss, J. (2016, Summer). *Where are all the teachers of color?* Retrieved from https://www.gse.harvard.edu/news/ed/16/05/where-are-all-teachers-color.

New York State Education Department. (2019a). *Front Street Elementary School at a glance*. Retrieved from https://data.nysed.gov/profile.php?instid=800000049867.

New York State Education Department. (2019b). *New York State culturally responsive-sustaining education framework*. Retrieved from http://www.nysed.gov/common/nysed/files/programs/crs/culturally-responsive-sustaining-education-framework.pdf.

New York University, Metropolitan Center for Urban Education. (2008, October). *Culturally responsive classroom management strategies.* Retrieved from https://research.steinhardt.nyu.edu/scmsAdmin/uploads/005/121/Culturally%20Responsive%20Classroom%20Mgmt%20Strat2.pdf.

Ordway, D. (2017, May 22). *Minority teachers: How students benefit from having teachers of same race.* Retrieved from https://journalistsresource.org/studies/society/education/minority-teachers-students-same-race-research/.

Rosenthal, R., & Jacobson, L. (1968). Pygmalion in the classroom. *The Urban Review, 3,* 16–20. https://doi.org/10.1007/BF02322211.

Schott Foundation. (2014, March). *Restorative practices: Fostering healthy relationships & promoting positive discipline in schools: A guide for educators.* Retrieved from http://schottfoundation.org/sites/default/files/restorative-practices-guide.pdf.

Smith, D., Fisher, D., & Frey, N. (2015). *Better than carrots or sticks: Restorative practices for positive classroom management.* ASCD.

Smith, N. L. (2020, December). *What are restorative justice circles, and when can they be utilized?* Retrieved from https://xqsuperschool.org/rethinktogether/restorative-justice-circles.

Stanford Center for Assessment, Learning, and Equity (SCALE). (2018). *edTPA: Understanding rubric level progressions.* Retrieved from https://www.tntech.edu/education/pdf/tk20/edtpa-urlp/edtpa-urlp-ell.pdf.

Stanford Center for Assessment, Learning, and Equity (SCALE). (2019). *edTPA: Elementary education: Literacy with mathematics task.* Retrieved from https://secure.aacte.org/apps/rl/resource.php?ref= edtpa#print.

Taylor, M. D. (1976). *Roll of thunder, hear my cry.* Penguin Random House.

Thomas, A. (2017). *The hate u give.* Harper Collins.

U.S. Department of Education. (2016). *The state of racial diversity in the educator workforce.* Policy and Program Studies Service Office of Planning, Evaluation, and Policy Development. Retrieved from https://www2.ed.gov/rschstat/eval/highered/racial-diversity/state-racial-diversity-workforce.pdf.

Wachtel, T. (2005, November). *The next step: Developing restorative communities.* Paper presented at the Seventh International Conference on Conferencing, Circles and other Restorative Practices, Manchester, UK.

Wachtel, T. (2013). *Defining restorative.* Retrieved from https://www.iirp.edu/pdf/Defining-Restorative.pdf.

Wachtel, T., & McCold, P. (2004). *From restorative justice to restorative practices: Expanding the paradigm.* Retrieved from https://www.iirp.edu/news/from-restorative-justice-to-restorative-practices-expanding-the-paradigm.

Weinstein, C., Curran, M., & Tomlinson-Clarke, S. (2003). Culturally responsive classroom management: Awareness into action. *Theory into Practice, 42*(4), 269–76. Retrieved from http://www.jstor.org/stable/1477388.

Wong, H. K., Wong, R. T., Jondahl, S. F., & Ferguson, O. F. (2018). *The classroom management book.* Harry K. Wong.

Woodson, J. (2018). *The day you begin.* Nancy Paulsen Books.

Workman, E. (2012, December). Teacher expectations for students: A self-fulfilling prophecy? *Progress of Education Reform, 23*(6), 1–7. Education Commission of the States. Retrieved from http://www.ecs.org/clearinghouse/01/05/51/10551.pdf.

Wright, S. P., Horn, S. P., & Sanders, W. L. (1997). Teacher and classroom context effects on student achievement: Implications for teacher evaluation. *Journal of Personnel Evaluation in Education, 11*, 57–67. https://doi.org/10.1023/A:1007999204543.

Personalizing Learning for Classroom Management

An *Evolution*

Maggie Blair and Kevin Sheehan

Benjamin Herold, a staff writer for *Education Week*, described the focus of *personalized learning* as the ability to "customize the learning experience for each student according to his or her unique skill, abilities, preferences, background, and experiences" (Herold, 2019, para. 4).

Although *personalized learning* is a current trend in the educational landscape, it is not a new concept. *Personalized learning* is anchored in the Progressive Education movement that dates back to European pedagogical reforms from the seventeenth through the nineteenth centuries. Indeed, John Dewey, considered the Father of Progressive Education, was a pragmatic progressivist who believed that students' interests should drive instruction (Dewey, 1938; Howlett & Cohan, 2016). Although there exist both pros and cons for Progressive Education (National Center for Learning Disabilities, 2020), one thing is for certain: When students are actively engaged in the learning process, classroom management is focused on instruction. In fact, classroom management is embedded into unit/lesson planning when educators customize the learning experience for each student according to his or her unique skill, abilities, preferences, background, and experiences.

As special education expanded from its inception into the arena of public education in 1975 with the passage of the Education for All Handicapped Children Act, to the passage of the Individuals with the Disabilities Education Act in 1990, 1997, and 2004, special education became a pioneer of personalized learning in the twenty-first century.

Education soon found the growing need to address another population of diverse students: ESOL learners. Both special education and ESOL presented instructional challenges for researchers, administrators, teachers, and students. In response, the field of special education incorporated assessments, classification requirements, and the implementation of Individual Education Plans (IEPs). IEPs identified specific benchmark goals for students and provided some guidance to school personnel on accommodations and modifications that would support the classified student in the general education classroom.

Thus began the next era of personalized learning that evolved from the Progressive Education movement.

PERSONALIZED LEARNING: INSTRUCTIONAL PLANNING

Mindset

Today, an "extraordinary teacher" is one who respects students' diversity and can effectively facilitate learning to achieve student understanding by recognizing and addressing each student's unique abilities, interests, needs, and cultural identity. This individual fosters critical, socially engaged intelligence that enables students to understand and ultimately participate collaboratively in their community (Dewey, 1938). Therefore, to be a truly effective "facilitator of learning," a teacher must become a keen observer of one's students, to not only recognize each student's unique gifts and challenges but also embrace and address these during instruction.

Oftentimes, educators rely on labels to define a student. Students are referred to as "average," "typically developing," "dyslexic," or "ESOL." What do any of these labels really mean? One student with a diagnosis of autism spectrum disorder (ASD) would look very different from another student with the same diagnosis. When a student with a diagnosis of attention deficit hyperactivity disorder (ADHD) enters a classroom, what might be the teacher's initial thoughts? Does the teacher have any idea that this student has the potential to be a team builder, a leader, a questioner, or a risk taker when no one else is willing to try something new or start a brainstorming session?

Current brain research (e.g., Shaywitz, 2020) is now changing special education jargon from a focus on "disabilities" to a focus on individual "differences" and "diversity." Old biases need to be revisited, researched, and redefined. The same is true for the growing population of culturally and linguistically diverse students. Therefore, the effective "facilitator of learning" in a personalized learning environment must begin his or her commitment to students by reflecting on previously held ideas and labels, while nurturing a more global, growth mindset when planning instruction for a community of diverse learners.

UNDERSTANDING BY DESIGN: PROCESSES

Where does one begin to plan instruction for diverse twenty-first-century classrooms? We might begin by looking at the groundbreaking work of Grant Wiggins and Jay McTighe, who turned the traditional model of classroom instruction on its head in 1998 with their groundbreaking work on teaching for understanding rather than on teaching for content coverage. Their seminal work, *Understanding by Design* (Wiggins & McTighe, 2005), proposed that the goal of student learning was to have the students, not the teachers, uncover the curriculum.

Their simple paradigm shift in personalized learning inspired a new framework for instructional planning that has the power to make classroom management an outgrowth of the student engagement that emerges from the content rather than as a matter of a teacher's control over classroom behaviors (Wiggins & McTighe, 2005).

At the core of their paradigm shift was the belief that teachers must first understand what it is that they want students to understand before they teach a single lesson. The word *understand* throws off most beginning teachers, but it is the key to the whole process. Wiggins and McTighe (2005) have not suggested that a teacher simply has to know the content, for that is easily accessible in the curriculum handbook or syllabus. At the heart of *Understanding by Design* is the central foundation that understanding is far more than just knowing.

Understanding requires that teachers plunge deeply into what they intend to teach to discover the big ideas that will drive the unit. The nonnegotiable driving principle of "understanding by design" suggests that if the teacher does not know what he or she hopes students will understand, there is little or no chance that the students ever will. The "by design" part of "Understanding by Design" is the payoff. Once a teacher knows what students should understand at the end of a lesson or a unit, the planning becomes easy, and the teacher can assure that every lesson is designed to lead to that end goal of the desired understanding.

Wiggins and McTighe (2005) proposed that the understanding rarely happens by accident but instead results from intense planning and design by teachers who truly know the end goal of what they hope students will understand. In helping teachers to move beyond knowing to the realm of understanding, Wiggins and McTighe (2005) proposed that there are six facets of understanding and that truly understanding a concept is far more than knowing or being able to recall the definition of a concept: When students truly understand a concept, they can (1) explain it, (2) interpret it, (3) apply it,

(4) have perspective on it, (5) have empathy for those involved, and (6) have self-knowledge of their own understanding (Wiggins & McTighe, 2005).

If students are to understand, the teacher must design lessons that provide them experiences in each of these facets. Figure 4.1 presents a visual representation of Wiggins and McTighe's (2005) three stages of "understanding by design."

Figure 4.1 most simply translates the Understanding by Design (UbD) framework and makes understandable the concept of "backwards design" that is at the heart of this curriculum planning model. The first step, *identify desired results*, asks teachers to wrestle with the content to determine the big ideas or idea that they hope students will understand at the end of the unit.

These big ideas are built on the discreet facts and skills that make up the unit. Student acquisition of basic facts and skills does not, however, guarantee true student understanding. The big ideas of a unit are what is important and timeless about those facts. Once teachers know what they want students to truly understand in a unit of study, step one of the Backwards Design planning process, *identify desired results*, has been accomplished. The design of the unit now has focus and purpose and opens opportunities for creating component lesson plans. This way of designing a unit can be as exciting for teachers in planning as it is for students in learning.

Backwards Design truly begins to take shape in step two: *determine acceptable evidence* (assessment). When teaching for understanding, a paper-and-pencil test may not be able to provide acceptable evidence. Even an essay may not measure which students, if any, truly understand the big idea.

Once the understanding and the evidence of that understanding are in place, then step three, *plan learning experience and instruction* (creation of the actual lessons), can commence. This model flips traditional curriculum planning in which teachers plan the lessons and then the assessment. Teachers will find that every lesson now has purpose on the path to understanding, but more importantly, students can also see the purpose of every lesson.

Often, evidence of understanding takes the form of a performance-based assessment in which students are required to demonstrate understanding in ways that far exceed meeting generic standards. Not only does this type of

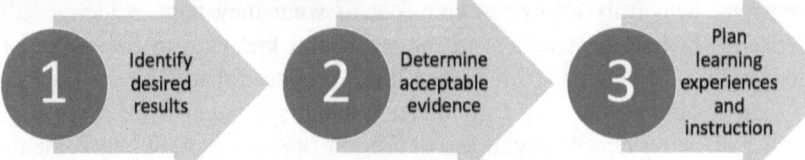

Figure 4.1 Understanding by design: Backwards design.
Source: Adapted from Wiggins and McTighe (2005).

assessment lead to more student engagement, but it also demands the curriculum be open to differentiation and involves group interaction and participation (Tomlinson & McTighe, 2006).

What most motivates students through the daily lessons is the thrill of the performance at the end of the unit. Similar to thespians preparing for a show or athletes practicing for a game, students will come to look on daily instruction as vital to their performance, and when well planned, these units can become lifelong memories that will be recalled decades later.

Practical Suggestions for Teachers: Planning an understanding-based unit.

Let's follow a fourth-grade team of teachers that designed a unit of study on the causes of the American Revolution.

The planning team of teachers began with the syllabus and content understandings of the grade level as defined by the state and school district. This team understood that the UbD curriculum planning model does not undermine the state curriculum but rather addresses and supports it.

Once the teachers identified the established curriculum content according to the state syllabus, they made a simplified list of what students had to know and be able do at the end of this unit. This opening list for the American Revolution centered on a list of laws and actions by the British government in their effort to collect more taxes from the colonies and the list of protests and counteractions by the colonists that led to the eventual conflict and ended with the colonies seeking independence. At this grade level, the state curriculum emphasis was on causes and outcomes.

After identifying the desired outcomes for this unit of study, the teachers began to discuss and creatively design learning experiences and assessments that would provide evidence of students' ability to apply the six facets of understanding to the causes and outcomes of the American Revolution. Some learning experiences included the following:

1. Finding a song or poem that captured the spirit of the revolution (Interpretation);
2. Encouraging students to discuss their limited roles in deciding school policy and comparing their feelings with those taxed without representation (Application and Empathy);
3. Reading documents from different points of view (Perspective); and
4. Creating political cartoons to summarize students' positions on why the final declaration of war was determined (Demonstration of Self-Knowledge).

As the teachers unleashed their creativity in this process, they began to immerse themselves into the concepts as historians and developed a deeper understanding of the American Revolution themselves.

The next step was vital and at the very heart of the unit design. The teachers engaged in deep discussions on how the original list of taxes by the British and grievances by the colonists led to a revolution. While the teachers found no one right answer, they did finally agree that the revolution was the result of a compromise failure.

As they began to see the events unfold as well as the consistent failure to compromise, the "big idea" that the American Revolution was caused by a failure to compromise came into focus for this team of teachers and ultimately drove the unit, connecting all the disparate facts in the syllabus. This "big idea" became the "desired results," the one idea that teachers hoped students would understand relating to the revolution and to any conflict that they might later encounter in school or life.

The teachers agreed that this "big idea" provided a truly engaging and timeless connection to their students' lives today as it did in 1776 and, more importantly, provided the team with an essential question that tied together the big idea and the desired results of the unit: "Could the American Revolution have been avoided?" This question was posed on the first day of the unit, so their students began their journey knowing the final question to be answered at the end of the unit.

Finally, the team of teachers decided that the best way to demonstrate evidence of understanding for this unit would be to have students engage in a simulated meeting of the key American protesters and British political figures attempting to come to a compromise. Some students were assigned specific character roles for the performance while other students contributed their unique skills in technology, art, music, or writing. All students contributed to this final performance, and they prepared for the meeting with all the fervor of any performance or athletic competition. Parents were invited to the auditorium to see and participate in their students' performance assessment.

At the end of the performance, a compromise was proposed, and each student and parent got to vote to demonstrate understanding. Of course, entrenched in their character and steeped in the history, there was ultimately a failure of the characters to compromise. There was, however, a deep understanding of the causes of the Revolution fostered in every student.

The above example of planning an understanding-based unit provides readers with an authentic sense of how successful understanding-based units evolve. It also focuses attention on the fact that UbD is an instructional framework anchored in the belief that instruction and planning should be student-centered and focused on student learning and understanding. This example affirms that the Backwards Design framework requires deliberate planning.

All materials selected for specific courses, units of study, and individual lessons must ultimately support students as they work toward achieving understanding through their mastery of specific goals. Once this plateau is reached, we soon realize how often classroom teachers begin planning a unit or lesson by identifying the topic to be covered and thinking about how they will "teach" the lesson or "cover" the topic, usually focusing on teacher-centered activities to move the lesson to closure.

We can professionally acknowledge that this very common process ultimately ends with a teacher-centered learning experience in which the teacher is the "sage onstage" rather than the "guide at the side" (King, 1993). This affirms that, in most instructional planning, little thought is given to three critical questions: (1) What do I want my students to know? (2) What do I want my students to truly understand? and (3) What do I want my students to be able to do at the end of this course/unit lesson?

In The Understanding by Design Framework Guide, McTighe and Wiggins (2012) elaborated on each planning stage by providing essential questions to guide decision-making and effective planning as follows:

Stage 1: Goal Setting—What should students know, understand, and be able to do? What big ideas are worthy of understanding and implied in the established goals (e.g., content standards, curriculum objectives, etc.)? What "enduring" understandings are desired? What provocative questions are worth pursuing to guide student inquiry into these big ideas? What specific knowledge and skills are targeted in the goals and needed for effective performance?

Stage 2: Goal Mastery—Assessment—This is where the evidence of learning is considered. How will we know if students have achieved the desired results and met the content standards? How will we know that students really understand the identified big ideas? What will we accept as evidence of proficiency?

Stage 3: Planning Learning Experiences and Instruction—With the learning goals set and appropriate evidence of understanding identified, facilitators of learning can now effectively plan learning experiences. What needs to be taught and coached? How should information be presented in light of the performance goals? In what order is information presented? In addition, when developing effective, student-centered instruction, an overall "master plan," inclusive of "long-term goals" supported by "smaller, short-term goals" that are aligned with meaningful periodic "assessments," is mandatory.

When the instructional planning begins by identifying the desired learning outcomes, we are better able to uncover potential obstacles that students might encounter on their academic journey and begin to analyze and explore a variety of solutions to ensure that all students have opportunities to both learn and demonstrate a successful mastery of all identified learning goals.

Therefore, student-centered planning begins by crafting instructional objectives for the learning outcomes: long-term and short-term goals. These instructional objectives are generally anchored in mandated curricula and must be written in behavioral terms. "Behavioral" indicates that outcomes must be observable and measurable, assessed by actions, and therefore, all instructional objectives must utilize observable and measurable action verbs.

A rich resource for action verbs is Bloom's Taxonomy, which in addition to providing verbs, has placed verbs in a hierarchy of mastery levels based on critical-thinking skills. This hierarchy is often helpful when delineating and refining students' mastery levels based on developmental levels, cognitive levels, social-emotional levels, and cultural/linguistic levels.

UNIVERSAL DESIGN FOR LEARNING

UbD is an instructional framework that has effectively questioned the most common approaches used by teachers when planning instruction and challenged them to rethink how they plan instruction as well as how they define their role in the classroom. However, does UbD as a "stand-alone" pedagogy address the student diversity in classrooms across the United States in the twenty-first century? At this time in history, perhaps the last question in UbD stage three might be reframed to ask this: How will we make learning both engaging and effective given the goals, the needed evidence, and the diversity of the learners?

When educators' mindsets move them beyond a dependency on labels to profile students, they come to value not only the importance of becoming keen observers of their students but also the strengths and talents that each student brings to the classroom community. Current research in the special education field is transforming a once deficit-driven arena into a more positive and inclusive learning environment driven by the belief that all students can learn, are entitled to a rigorous and respectful academic curricula, and should be planfully supported as they engage in the learning process.

Universal Design for Learning (UDL), another instructional framework, originally emerged from the architectural concept of "Universal Design," in which products and/or environments are designed to make them accessible to all people to the greatest extent possible regardless of age, physical needs, and other factors.

The term universal design was first coined by architect Ronald Mace (Center for Disability Rights, n.d.), who himself contracted polio at the age of nine and spent the rest of his life in a wheelchair. He was an early advocate for building accessibility for all, and his professional work, along with his advocacy skills, impacted such federal legislation as the Fair Housing Amendments Act of 1988 and the Americans with Disabilities Act of 1990.

Universal Design for Learning is a scientifically designed framework for improving and optimizing curriculum design and instructional practices for all learners. Like the architectural focus of Universal Design, Universal Design for Learning is focused on accessibility—accessibility to teaching and learning environments.

The Center for Applied Special Technology (CAST) has researched and expanded the field of Universal Design for Learning since its founding in 1984. CAST has also been responsible for the successful development of the UDL framework that effectively links current research in brain-based learning with current research and design of new technology. Since its founding in 1984, CAST's mission has been "to transform education design and practice until learning has no limits" (CAST, 2021a, para. 1).

Its history has been uniquely aligned to the evolution of a Free Appropriate Public Education for special education students in general education classrooms. Over the years, CAST has developed real-time applications of personalized learning experiences to meet the challenges that diverse learners face in general education classrooms. Brain-based research has identified three neural networks that impact learning: the Recognition Networks, the Strategic Networks, and the Affective Networks.

The Recognition Networks are located in the back of the brain and enable learners to identify and assign meaning to patterns identified by their senses from simple patterns like facial and voice recognition to understanding more complex patterns as cause-and-effect relationships. The Recognition Networks are the what of learning.

The Strategic Networks, located in the front of the brain, enable learners to plan, execute, and monitor their actions. The Strategic Networks are the how of learning.

The Affective Networks, located in the center of the brain, evaluate and assign emotional significance to patterns and situations experienced by the individual. These networks enable individuals to engage in the world around them. For students, this is the world of teaching and learning. The impact of the Affective Networks is critical to student motivation and sustained engagement in the learning process. The Affective Network directs the why of learning.

Table 4.1 illustrates how the UDL framework addresses these three major networks when planning and implementing classroom instruction (CAST, 2016, 2018a, 2018b).

Universal Design for Learning is an approach to teaching and learning anchored in the belief that all students can actively participate in and successfully achieve mastery of instructional goals when provided with equal learning opportunities. Therefore, the overarching goal of UDL is to provide "facilitators of learning" with a rich variety of instructional strategies to remove potential engagement barriers from their students (CAST, 2021b).

In 2006, representatives from leading educational and disability organizations across the United States formed the National Universal Design for Learning Taskforce (CAST, 2021b). The goal of this group was to expand awareness of UDL as a teaching and learning approach among national, state, and local policy makers.

Table 4.1 Universal Design for Learning: An Effective Planning Tool

Network	Description	Process	Strategies
Recognition Network	Identifies and assigns meaning to patterns	The *what* of learning: How do students gather information?	Provide multiple means of *representation*: • Provide multiple multi-modal examples • Highlight critical facts or features • Provide multiple media and presentation formats • Support background context
Strategic Network	Supports planning, execution, and monitoring of actions	The *how* of learning: How do students plan and perform tasks? How do students organize thought and express ideas?	Provide multiple means of *action* and *expression*: • Provide flexible models of skilled performance • Provide opportunities to practice with support • Provide ongoing, relevant feedback • Offer flexible opportunities to demonstrate skill
Affective Network	Supports learner motivation, engagement, challenges, interests, and excites students	This is the *why* of learning: How do teachers encourage students to actively engage in the learning process?	Provide multiple means of *engagement*: • Offer choices of content and tools • Provide adjustable levels of challenge • Offer choices for assessments • Provide a variety of learning activities and groupings

It is interesting to note that the formation of this taskforce occurred two years after the last federal reauthorization of the Individuals with Disabilities Education Act of 2004. This act had required states and local educational districts to provide struggling students with research-based interventions and close monitoring of these interventions prior to making a referral for special education services—in other words, to provide a more personal approach to instruction for students who learn differently.

In 2016, CAST introduced its most recent version of UDL Guidelines. In this updated set of UDL Guidelines, the Affective Network (Engagement) has been placed in the first column "emphasizing its essential role in the perception and strategic action necessary for learning" (CAST, 2016, para. 1).

This revision also reiterates the importance of the individual in the learning process and issues the ultimate mandate to all educators to "personalize" instruction to meet the strengths and challenges of all students. The overarching goal of the current UDL Guidelines is to foster "expert learners who are: 1) purposeful and motivated, 2) resourceful and knowledgeable, and 3) strategic and goal-directed." The full version of the UDL Guidelines is available at CAST (2018a).

Practical Suggestions for Teachers

The Universal Design for Learning framework is a powerful tool when developing the scope and sequence of a unit or an individual lesson plan. Since long-term and short-term goals have been clarified through the lens of UDL, the next step in planning is determining students' collective and individual appropriate points of entry for the content to be presented.

Critical entry point questions to ask include the following: What prior knowledge must students already have about the topic? What skills must students have mastered to explore the topic? What vocabulary on this topic will be new to students? What new skill sets will be required for students to successfully meet mastery of the designated instructional objective? These questions can guide motivational activities for individual lessons within the unit.

By focusing on the Affective Networks (the why of learning), we can deliberately design motivational activities that engage students and draw them into the learning process while providing teachers with valuable information on students' strengths and challenges relating to the specific topic. Data collected during motivational activities can provide guidance when developing the scope and sequence of the ensuing lessons. While curricula standards are set by federal, state, and institutional mandates, students certainly drive the planning.

The effectiveness of any individual lesson is anchored in (1) the organized and sequential dissemination of new content and (2) the fidelity of assessment and monitoring of student progress. Developmental procedures must reflect thoughtful planning to appropriately pace instruction, assessment, scaffolding activities, and transitions throughout the instructional segment. The Recognition Networks (the what of learning) and the Strategic Networks (the how of learning) provide guidance and support for the creation and design of effective developmental procedures (CAST, 2018b).

DIFFERENTIATED INSTRUCTION

Differentiation means tailoring instruction to meet individual needs. Whether teachers differentiate content, process, products, or the learning environment, the use of ongoing assessment and flexible grouping makes this a successful approach to instruction. Tomlinson (2001) maintained that "Differentiated instruction is dynamic; Teachers monitor the match between the learner and learning to make adjustments as warranted" (p. 5). Therefore, to effectively differentiate instruction, educators need to observe and identify the similarities and differences among students and then creatively use this information to effectively plan more personalized instruction.

Differentiated instruction as a teaching theory is based on the premise that instructional approaches should vary and be adapted to meet the needs of both individual and diverse students in a classroom. The intent of this student-centered approach to instruction is to maximize each student's growth and individual success. It recognizes and values each learner and therefore encourages and supports each student to become an active member of the learning process.

Differential instruction recognizes and responds responsively to four critical student facets: (1) prior knowledge, (2) skill readiness, (3) language and culture, and (4) learning preferences. Differentiated instruction is not only for students who learn differently or for culturally/linguistically diverse students; rather, it is for every student in the learning community.

The Learning Cycle offers a comprehensive road map for teachers planning instruction (see figure 4.2). It initially appeared in a report on "Differentiated Instruction: Effective Classroom Practices Report" (Hall, 2002). The report outlined the comprehensive development of a unit, learning segment, or a lesson plan from the Pre-Assessment (Motivational) Stage through to Summative Evaluation Stage (Assessment of Long-Term Instructional Goal) and is anchored in the seminal work of Carol Ann Tomlinson and the CAST organization.

The Learning Cycle graphic of figure 4.2 highlights three areas that can be effectively differentiated: (a) Content, (b) Process, and (c) Product. Content identifies what the teacher plans to teach. Process identifies how the teacher

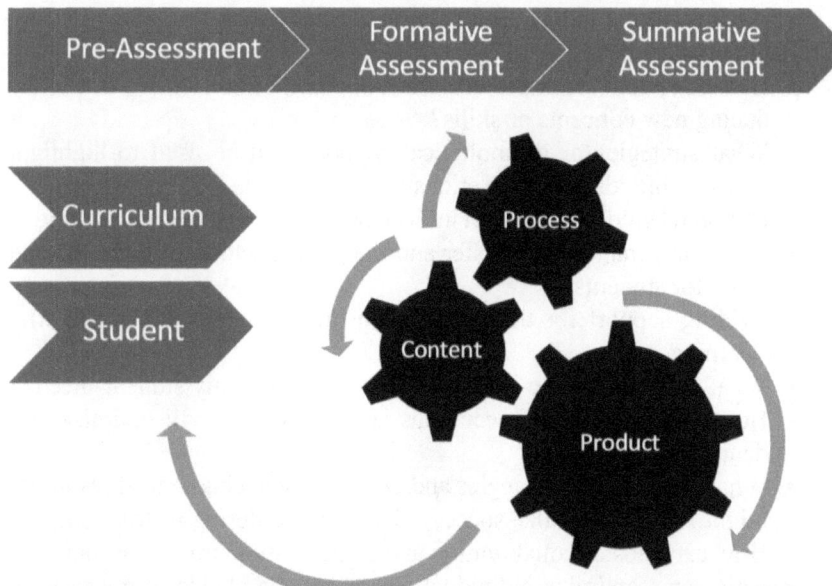

Figure 4.2 The Learning Cycle.
Source: Adapted from Oaksford and Jones (2001).

plans to facilitate the instruction. Product identifies how the teacher plans to assess. The Content reflects the instructional goal, the Process reflects the procedural development, and the Product reflects the assessment artifacts.

Practical Suggestions for Teachers

As previously discussed, the UDL framework has consistently been anchored in current and ongoing brain-based research (Jensen, 2008) that has identified three brain networks that support learning: Affective Networks that support student engagement, Recognition Networks that support content representation, and Strategic Networks that support student action and expression. The UDL Guidelines 2.2 Graphic Organizer is the most current version of UDL Guidelines (CAST, 2018a). These guidelines provide educators with powerful suggestions for designing differentiated units and segments of study or individual lesson plans that make the content readily accessible to all students.

To support differentiated instruction, CAST proposed in the UDL Guidelines (2018a) the following three categories:

1. Providing support for the Recognition Networks: The what of learning
   - How can I customize informational learning displays that introduce, explain, and/or review new concepts and skills for diverse learners?

- What auditory and/or visual alternatives might be available to struggling students?
- How can I activate or provide relevant context knowledge when introducing new concepts or skills?
- What strategies or technological supports can be used to highlight patterns, big ideas, and relationships for students?
- How can I guide and support information processing and visualization?
- How can I maximize transfer and the generalization of concepts and skills for students?

2. Providing support for the Affective/Engagement Networks: The why of learning
   - What personal coping skills and strategies might my students need?
   - How can I promote expectations and beliefs that will optimize students' motivation?
   - What instructional strategies and/or in-person/technological resources might I use to optimize successful challenges during instruction?
   - How can I foster collaboration and community in my classroom?
   - How can I optimize individual autonomy and choice in my instructional segments?
   - How can I foster relevance and authenticity in the learning process?

3. Providing support for the Strategic Networks: The how of learning
   - How can I vary student response methods to ensure that every student has an opportunity to share information?
   - What high-tech and low-tech instructional technologies or assistive technologies should be incorporated in the lessons to ensure interactive student participation?
      a. What types of multimedia can be used during instruction and assessment?
      b. What types of nontechnological tools might be used by students to construct or create authentic responses and products?
   - How can I support planning and strategy development with my students?
   - How can I improve my students' abilities to manage information and resources?
   - How can I encourage self-monitoring with my students?

The responses to all of the above questions are best determined by how well the "facilitator of instruction" (i.e., the teacher) has come to know his or her students.

CO-TEACHING

Often, school districts assign pairs of faculty members to inclusion classes based on their certification and licensure. When approached in this way, co-teaching becomes a teaching assignment rather than a teaching experience. According to the CAST Professional Publishing site, "Co-teaching is the practice of pairing teachers together in a classroom to share the responsibilities of planning, instructing and assessing students" (Mihai, 2021).

Professional equity is one of the most critical elements in effective co-taught classrooms. As mentioned earlier in this chapter, special education has been a pioneer in the arena of personalized learning in the twenty-first century. The pairing of a general education/content-specific teacher with a special educator in one classroom has been the common practice in many school districts across the country since the mid-1990s (Cook & Friend, 1995).

Many districts have also used the practice of co-teaching in ESOL classes. However, in recent years, when allocating personnel within school districts, oftentimes, the "cost" per pupil overrides the "quality of education" per pupil. When decisions are made solely on finances, the practice of co-teaching becomes, at best, a teaching assignment and, at worst, a worthless attempt to respond to legal mandates for students' rights to a free and appropriate public education.

The implementation of successful co-teaching models is challenging and requires change at many levels. In the conclusion of their article, "The Many Faces of Collaborative Planning and Teaching," Thousand et al. (2006) explored a "Triangle of Responsibility." This triangle includes the responsibilities of teacher preparation programs, school districts, and individual educators for preparing, supporting, and effectively implementing successful co-teaching teams.

Teacher preparation programs must be held accountable for providing not only training but also modeling of effective collaborative planning and teaching practices for all future educators. Furthermore, school district administrators must be held accountable for ongoing professional development, the provision of necessary resources (common planning and teaching times, opportunities to attend professionally relevant conferences), and meaningful evaluations and feedback to co-teaching teams. Co-teaching teams must be held accountable for developing and nurturing common goals, a shared belief system, an open and respectful system of communication, and a fair and equitable allocation of responsibilities, values, and support to all team members.

When co-teaching is implemented with integrity, it can yield several relevant classroom management benefits:

- Expanded opportunities for one-to-one instruction and coaching, which leads to stronger personal relationships between students and teachers.
- Expanded opportunities for diverse students to access their right to a free, appropriate public education, including their right to be included in rich, interactive, classroom communities and all school-sponsored activities.
- Expanded opportunities for all students to successfully access specialized instruction when needed.
- Expanded opportunities for all students to access more creative and engaging instruction, with lessons planned and facilitated by two professionals who possess unique training and prior experiences in a classroom.

In their publication, *Interactions: Collaboration Skills for School Professionals,* Friend and Cook (2000) discussed six approaches to co-teaching: (1) One Teach, One Assist; (2) One Teach, One Observe; (3) Station Teaching; (4) Parallel Teaching; (5) Alternative Teaching; and (6) Team Teaching.

One Teach, One Assist—In this model, one teacher is the primary instructor and the other teacher assists students by monitoring their independent work, answering their questions, providing necessary supplies and materials, providing behavioral support or interventions where necessary, and asking the lead teacher to clarify any misconceptions or directions.

One Teach, One Observe—In this model, which is used only occasionally, one teacher is the primary instructor and the other teacher gathers specific, observational information on students' academic, behavioral, and social skills.

Station Teaching—In this model, a class is divided into several small groups, each of which move from one station to another in the classroom. Specific instruction is delivered at each station. Activities at each station are designed to function independently of one another, and activities at all the tables require approximately the same amount of time. This model reduces the student—teacher ratio, increases student engagement, and provides effective monitoring of students' progress.

Parallel Teaching—Co-teachers divide the class into two groups, and each teacher provides instruction to one of the two groups. Students remain in the same group for the duration of the lesson. This model enables teachers to maximize direct instruction to students while encouraging and supporting student participation. When using this model, co-teachers must have adequate space in which to work as well as the availability of any required technology. This model also requires co-teachers to be cognizant of potential audio and visual distractors as well as time management.

Alternative Teaching—This model is sometimes referred to as Differentiated Teaching. In this model, one teacher works with a large group of students while the co-teacher provides specific instruction to a small group of students. This model is often used when providing enrichment, remediation, and pre-teaching activities. It can also be used as an alternate method of providing support to specific students during certain learning experiences.

Team Teaching—This is the model where both teachers share direct instruction. They are equally active in the facilitation of instruction. Although most people feel this is the "highest level" of co-teaching, this model should not be used frequently because when two individuals in lead positions are engaged in whole-class instruction, subtle needs of students are not always recognized nor adequately addressed in a timely fashion.

The re-authorization of the Individuals with Disabilities Education Act of 2004 mandated that individuals with disabilities have the right to participate in a general education curriculum and be ensured the right to "specially designed instruction" as prescribed in a student's Individualized Education Plan. Furthermore, in her article "Welcome to Co-Teaching 2.0," Marilyn Friend (2015) defined specially designed instruction as instruction that relates to all academic, organizational, vocational, behavioral, and communicative instruction related to the achievement of IEP goals. Specially designed instruction supports instructional changes in content (but not standards), methodology, and instructional delivery, as well as the use of approaches and techniques not required by other learners.

Although specially designed instruction is not the same as differentiation of instruction, this was what special education teachers were required to do to ensure that students reached their IEP goals. This 2004 special education mandate, along with the subsequent work of educational researchers such as Grant Wiggins and Jay McTighe (UbD), CAST (UDL), and Carol Ann Tomlinson (ID), eventually generated a broader awareness of the need to expand personalized instruction to a broader student population.

Friend (2015) also put forth a timely revision of her initial co-teaching models to more precisely address meeting the current needs of special education students. She discussed a once-critical goal for novice co-teaching teams: building strong, professional relationships. She indicated that this initial focus on team building ultimately diverted co-teaching teams from several other goals that were equally important for student success.

During the early years of co-teaching, as teams worked on aspects of team-building, they continued to use "the general education curriculum as the basis for their shared work" and continued to measure student mastery by improved performance on high-stake assessments. According to Friend (2015), the most critical activity that co-teachers gave up during the early days of co-teaching was attention to the unique needs of students and the personalized instruction necessary to meet those needs.

Furthermore, Friend went on to discuss how current co-teachers can effectively integrate specifically designed instruction into several of her original co-teaching models. By 2015, many teacher preparation programs, school districts across the country, and classroom teachers (including co-teachers) had begun to explore UbD and UDL frameworks to see how to effectively differentiate content, product, and process for all students.

Although classified students' IEPs often provided some guidance, most classroom teachers, including co-teachers, were now challenged to expand collaboration to related service providers, content area specialists, and ESOL teachers to successfully reach and engage all diverse learners in their classrooms. All teachers were now successfully providing the same kind of individually designed and carefully documented instruction that had always characterized special education—personalized learning.

Table 4.2 identifies student needs, strategies to support instruction, examples of a specific strategy, the individual on a co-teaching team who might be responsible for the implementation of the strategy, and the co-teaching models that can support these actions.

Practical Suggestions for Teachers

Despite current concerns about the costs per pupil, co-teaching can be a very practical approach when meeting diversity needs of twenty-first-century American classrooms. Previously, this chapter introduced the Learning Cycle and identified the three areas where differentiation of instruction is particularly effective: Content (the what of teaching), Process (the how of teaching), and Product (the how of assessment). Effective co-teaching practices support differentiation, particularly in the areas of Process and Product.

One Teach, One Observe Model. At first blush, this approach may seem nonrelevant to instruction, but it is a critical model when getting to know students' strengths and challenges that offer the data required to meaningfully provide accommodations, modifications, and choices to students for both instruction and assessment.

This model is most successful when both teachers equally share the "teach" and "observe" roles in which neither takes on the mantle of "teacher" or

Table 4.2. Co-teaching models supporting specifically designed instruction.

Student Needs	Co-Teaching Model	Strategy	Example	Explanation
Struggle with wait time	• One Teach, One Assist • Station Teaching • Parallel Teaching • Alternate Teaching	Embedding a behavioral strategy into instruction	Social Stories	One teacher is responsible for scripting, introducing, and post-ing a Social Story for the student to reference and practice during instruction
Struggle with wait time	• One Teach, One Assist • Parallel Teaching • Alternate Teaching	Embedding a behavioral strategy into instruction	Token Economy	One teacher is responsible for providing the reinforcement tokens at set intervals during instruction
Struggle with new academic vocabulary	• Parallel Teaching • Alternative Teaching	Introducing and practicing new content vocabulary	• Pre-teaching activities • Special education teacher/Speech-language pathologist • ESL teacher • ESOL teacher	One teacher is responsible for identifying and teaching new vocabulary prior to the beginning of a new unit of study
Struggle to take notes	• One Teach, One Assist • One Teach, One Observe • Alternative Teaching	Embedding notetaking strategies into instruction	• Graphomotor and Keyboarding Skills • Occupational therapist	The occupational therapist consults with the classroom teacher to support generalizing skills in the classroom
Struggle to take notes	• One Teach, One Assist • One Teach, One Observe • Parallel Teaching • Alternative Teaching	Embedding notetaking strategies into instruction	• Organizational Skills • Use of Notetaking • Graphic Organizer • Special education teacher	The special education teacher is responsible for designing, introducing, and monitoring a note-taking graphic organizer for students
Struggle to identify fractional parts of a whole	• One Teach, One Assist • Station Teaching • Parallel Teaching • Alternative Teaching	Embedding concrete instructional materials into direct instruction	• Multi-sensory instruction • Providing students with visual cues and tactile experiences during direct instruction	The special education teacher is responsible for providing a variety of visual cues and manipulatives during instruction

This is an original table developed by the authors for the purpose of this chapter.

"support personnel." In addition, shared data-collection opportunities ensure data consistency through high interobserver agreement, and finally, the equal partnering of roles encourages rich dialogue during co-planning discussions.

The One Teach, One Observe Model is also very practical when collecting observational data as part of a Functional Behavior Assessment (discussed in detail in book 2, chapter 4). Oftentimes, classroom teachers partner with behavior consultants when students require specialized interventions, but for behavioral interventions to be successful, these itinerant consultants rely on input from classroom teachers for both initial data collection and the monitoring of student progress.

Alternative Teaching Model. Often referred to as Differentiated Teaching, the Alternative Teaching Model often includes professionals other than just co-teachers. This model relies on professional expertise from support personnel such as physical and occupational therapists, speech/language pathologists, behavior consultants, ESL teachers, and programmatic or one-to-one teacher assistants.

In Marilyn Friend's (2015) article, "Welcome to Co-Teaching 2.0," she pointed out that nowadays, co-teaching educators integrate special education strategies and techniques into daily lessons. This planful integration not only supports active learning but also enables classified students to achieve the goals of their IEP. Instead of depending on piecemeal prompting and coaching to get struggling students through the academic content, effective co-teachers now provide individually designed, carefully documented instruction that has always characterized special education. Special education has always been on the cutting edge of personalized learning.

One of the most successful ways to differentiate instruction is grouping, which can be random or specific to instruction. Random groups work best when the goal of the lesson is to identify student entry points for a particular unit of study or to brainstorm ideas. Teachers need a clear vision of their end goal prior to actually grouping students and should be able to answer the question: What is it that we want our students to truly understand? Or what do we want our students to be able to do?

For instructional purposes, there can be same-ability groups or mixed-ability groups. Same-ability groupings are successfully used when introducing new topics (including new vocabulary), new concepts, and new skill sets. Students in same-ability groups can be assigned an instructional facilitator based on similar strengths or similar areas of deficit. Instructional facilitators can be one of the co-teachers or a related service provider.

Mixed-ability groups are more successfully used when there is a focus on student collaboration throughout the learning process. This type of grouping can support students academically, social-emotionally, and behaviorally in the classroom. Groupings are most effectively used in the One Teach, One Assist model; Station Teaching; and Parallel Teaching.

Offering choices is another successful way to differentiate instruction. Providing students with different ways to access information, manipulate information, and successfully demonstrate the mastery of information empowers student success in the classroom. Again, providing meaningful choices is dependent on the co-teacher's ability to (1) identify the learning goals of the unit or lesson; (2) determine the acceptable assessment of mastery; and (3) plan a variety of learning experiences to take in (recognize) information, manipulate (strategize and assess) information, and ensure students' motivational and sustained engagement (affect) with information.

Choices can be successfully identified when practicing the co-teaching models of One Teach, One Assist as well as One Teach, One Observe. Choices can also be used to facilitate Station Teaching, Parallel Teaching, Alternative Teaching, and Team-Teaching models. To meaningfully provide choices, co-teachers must truly know and understand their students and have a clear vision of their long-term and short-term learning goals.

CONCLUSION

For early twenty-first-century educators, the term classroom management is a more complex combination of factors than it was even several decades ago. The student population is more diverse, and federal and state mandates require more dedicated attention to curriculum planning and monitoring students' ability to successfully meet state and local standards. There is also a greater availability of rich, brain-based research on how our brains work and why some students might struggle when learning to read or when reciprocal conversation is required. In addition, there has been an explosion of technological innovations to support students in classrooms.

All of the above impact the teacher's ability to manage a learning environment that is safe and structured as well as motivational and engaging for students. In the past, classroom management typically described a teacher-centered environment in which everyone did the same thing, at the same time, with the same results.

Today, classroom management refers to a student-centered learning environment where students are valued for their unique strengths and provided support when required. We now recognize that when students are actively motivated and engaged in the learning process, classroom management is no longer an additional factor in the teaching and learning process but rather something that is embedded into the very fiber of instructional planning.

Today, we proactively plan to reach our very diverse student populations. We begin the process by respectfully setting high expectations for all students' success. We then identify desired results and determine acceptable evidence of mastery for all students. As we plan learning experiences, we use brain-based research to design instruction that addresses the what of learning, the why of learning, and the how of learning.

These steps enable us to focus attention on our students' strengths and challenges in order to thoughtfully differentiate instruction and assessment so that each student is motivated and engaged in the learning process. Today, we refocus our attention from classroom management to personalized learning for all.

REFERENCES

CAST. (2016). *UDL tips for designing an engaging learning environment.* Retrieved from https://www.cast.org/products-services/resources/2016/udl-tips-designing-engaging-learning-environment.

CAST. (2018a). The universal design for learning guidelines, version 2.2. Retrieved from http://udlguidelines.cast.org.

CAST. (2018b). UDL and the learning brain. Retrieved from https://www.cast.org/products-services/resources/2018/udl-learning-brain-neuroscience.

CAST. (2021a). About CAST. Retrieved from http://www.cast.org/about/about-cast.

CAST. (2021b). More than 45 organizations work together to promote UDL in policy. Retrieved from https://www.cast.org/impact/work-stories/udl-national-task-force.

Center for Disability Rights. (n.d.). *Ronald Mace and his impact on universal design.* Retrieved from https://cdrnys.org/blog/advocacy/ronald-mace-and-his-impact-on-universal-design/.

Cook, L., & Friend, M. (1995). Co-teaching: Guidelines for creating effective practices. *Focus on Exceptional Children, 28*(3), 1. https://doi.org/10.17161/foec.v28i3.6852.

Dewey, J. (1938). *Experience and education.* Macmillan.

Friend, M. P. (2015). Welcome to co-teaching 2.0. *Educational Leadership, 73*(4), 16–22.

Friend, M. P., & Cook, L. (2000). *Interactions: Collaboration skills for school professionals.* New York: Longman.

Hall, T. (2002). *Differentiated instruction: Effective classroom practices report.* Retrieved from https://www.scirp.org/reference/ReferencesPapers.aspx?ReferenceID=2464879.

Herold, B. (2019, Nov. 5). *What is personalized learning?* Retrieved from https://www.edweek.org/technology/what-is-personalized-learning/2019/11.

Howlett, C. F., & Cohan, A. (2016). John Dewey: His role in public scholarship to educate for peace. *Social and Education History, 5*(3), 203–22. https://doi.org/10.17583/hse.2016.2097.

Jensen, E. P. (2008). A fresh look at brain-based education. *Phi Delt Kappan, 89*(6), 408–17. http://www.jstor.org/stable/20442521.

King, A. (1993). From sage on the stage to guide on the side. *College Teaching, 41*(1), 30–36.

McTighe, J., & Wiggins, G. (2012). *Understanding by design framework*. Association for Supervision and Curriculum Development. Retrieved from https://ascd.org/ASCD/pdf/siteASCD/publications/UbD_WhitePaper0312.pdf.

Mihai, A. (2021, Sept. 16). The power of two: Exploring co-teaching. *The Educationalist*. Retrieved from https://educationalist.substack.com/p/the-power-of-two-exploring-co-teaching.

National Center for Learning Disabilities. (2020). *Significant disproportionality in special education: Current trends and actions for impact*. Retrieved from https://www.ncld.org/wp-content/uploads/2020/10/2020-NCLD-Disproportionality_Trends-and-Actions-for-Impact_FINAL-1.pdf.

Oaksford, L., & Jones, L. (2001). *Differentiated instruction abstract*. Leon County Schools.

Shaywitz, S. E. (2020). *Overcoming dyslexia* (2nd ed.). Alfred A. Knopf.

Thousand, J. S., Villa, R. A., & Nevin, A. I. (2006). The many faces of collaborative planning and teaching. *Theory into Practice, 45*(3), 239–48. http://www.jstor.org/stable/40071603.

Tomlinson, C. A. (2001). *How to differentiate instruction in mixed-ability classrooms*. Association for Supervision and Curriculum Development.

Tomlinson, C. A., & McTighe, J. (2006). *Integrating differentiated instruction & understanding by design: Connecting content and kids*. Association for Supervision and Curriculum Development.

Wiggins, G. P., & McTighe, J. (2005). *Understanding by design* (2nd ed.). Association for Supervision and Curriculum Development.

Classroom Management for Culturally and Linguistically Diverse Learners

Carrie L. McDermott Goldman and Lisa A. Peluso

Classroom management refers to the environment of a classroom and the activities that build a positive climate for teaching and learning (Martin & Sugarman, 1993). The uniqueness of an individual, the recognition of our differences, and how we embrace them are the fundamental concepts of diversity. As classrooms across the United States become more diverse, the aforementioned concepts impact student success and overall outcomes. For the purposes of teaching and learning, the classroom environment is a place to affirm, value, and use cultural identities, including age, gender, language, religion, ability, socioeconomic background, sexuality, race, and ethnicity.

HISTORICAL OVERVIEW

Although the culture of the United States has been coined the "melting pot," diversity in American schools and classrooms has had a long and arduous road. This path can be traced back to the U.S. Founding Fathers and continues to be a challenge in educational institutions today. Brophy (2011) depicted classroom management as the means of creating a classroom climate that is conducive to learning. However, if a teacher is not willing to embrace student diversity, effective classroom management cannot take place.

In this chapter, we discuss historical-cultural perspectives of education in the United States, shifts of populations and how these impact classroom management, and fundamental concepts of cultural diversity and what they mean for today's classrooms.

The nation's third president, Thomas Jefferson, proposed a bill that would require the government to provide three years of gratis education to U.S.

citizens of all classes. Nonetheless, this legislation was not without its caveats. It was Jefferson's intention that this education be applied exclusively to "white, non-slave youth" (Huerta, 2009). Moreover, this bill was not intended for the female segment of the population nor Blacks or Native Americans. The bill itself was not passed, but its underpinnings of who should or should not be educated were revealed.

As outlined by Huerta (2009), Horace Mann sparked the next major movement in American education around 1837, with his notion of common schools, what would later become known as public schools. Mann viewed education as a means of creating good citizens and bolstering a burgeoning nation's economy.

Unlike Jefferson, he was in favor of educating African Americans, whether slave or not. However, the segregation of Black students in the northern states persisted throughout the early and mid-nineteenth century, with the case of *Roberts v. City of Boston* in 1855, which was the first law banning segregation in public schools. It would also be the cornerstone for *Plessy v. Ferguson*, rationalizing that separate could be equal (Bernard & Mondale, 2001).

In terms of classroom management in the nineteenth and early twentieth centuries, the most commonly used strategy was corporal punishment. Besides calling for state-funded education for a more diverse population, Horace Mann "argued vigorously . . . for the rejection of corporal punishment" (Huerta, 2009, p. 10). Thus, in addition to advocating for a more humane approach to teaching, Mann took into consideration the conditions of the school buildings, classrooms, and materials utilized, as he felt that all these factors contributed to students' ability or inability to learn (Bernard & Mondale, 2001). Although Mann is highly regarded for his educational reforms, there is another element of diversity and classroom management that he overlooked: religion.

During the first half of the nineteenth century, the United States received new groups of émigrés coming particularly from Ireland, France, and Germany. With their arrival, a new form of apprehension, suspicion, and subsequent persecution arose from those already established in this nation in the form of nativism or extreme ethnocentrism. The notion that all citizens were entitled to free and basic education was quite beneficial to all recipients, but the heavily Protestant-leaning curriculum and choice of materials utilized during this time were not.

A central text for all students' instruction was the Protestant King James Version of the Bible. This requirement led directly to this country's Bible Riots of the 1840s, as the majority of Catholic students compelled to interact with this work were Irish immigrants who had fled from British-Protestant domination and subjugation in their own nation (Caruso, 2012; Walch, 2003).

In addition, Walch noted the use of readers developed by William H. McGuffey, also known as the McGuffey Readers, as tools of instruction. The contents of these volumes were based on morals reflecting distinctly Protestant values. Walch (2003) pointed out that books such as these were used as homogenizers, trying to eradicate the foreignness from non-native Catholic students. Thus, a highly utilized classroom management tool was assimilation.

Beyond English-speaking Irish Catholic immigrants, ethnic diversity expanded in this country in at least two ways. As is most popularly known, American school populations grew exponentially vis-à-vis the Great Wave of Immigration in the latter part of the century, presenting the nation with an influx of Southern and Eastern Europeans. As well, there was an influx of Asian immigrants during the mid-nineteenth and early twentieth centuries.

Classroom management for the Europeans oftentimes translated as giving lessons in hygiene, tracking immigrant students for vocational studies, and retaining those who could not master the English language (Ravitch, 2001). Conversely, practices assisting immigrants in the assimilation process did vary on school and geographical location, with some schools offering a rudimentary form of bilingual education or night classes to meet the needs of working children.

Like their African American counterparts, Asian children living on the West Coast were compelled to attend segregated schools, with school superintendents considering students as "Mongolian," regardless of whether their descent was Chinese, Japanese, or Korean. As cited by the Asia Society (2019), in 1905, the San Francisco School Board stated, "Our children should not be placed in any position where their youthful impressions may be affected by association with pupils of the Mongolian race." Thus, it could be said that classroom management was based on fear and prejudice.

Bernard and Mondale (2001) pointed out that the advent of the Great Depression in 1929 through the 1930s contributed to larger numbers of students in American schools. This explosion in student population was because child labor laws went into effect, but also given the country's economic status, there were no jobs available for school-age children. Crowded general education classrooms prompted greater use of IQ tests for student tracking, and "by the 1930s, two-thirds of the Mexican-American students in Los Angeles were classified as slow learners, even mentally retarded" (Bernard & Mondale, 2001, p. 104).

This classification led to another form of diversity in American public schools: those of diverse academic and social abilities. Winzer (1993) maintained that educating exceptional children has been formally in existence since the late eighteenth century. Initially in North America, separate facilities were recommended for African Americans and Asians, with greater emphasis on education for the blind and the deaf.

Nevertheless, at the start of the twentieth century, "the focus of special education changed from isolated institutional settings to segregated classrooms within the public schools" (Winzer, 1993). It was also at this time the practice of "labeling" students (identifying students by ability, intelligence, need, class, race, etc.) began to develop in schools. Winzer (1993) maintained that although this categorization opened up educational resources to more children in need, labeling also segregated a larger number of children from the student body.

Advances have been made to recognize the needs of different types of learners and how to improve the quality of education through the passage of the Elementary and Secondary Education Act (ESEA) of 1965; Individuals with Disabilities Acts from 1990, 1997, and 2004, and its precursor of 1975 Education for All Handicapped Children Act; as well as the rulings from Lau v. Nichols in 1974.

With the reauthorization of ESEA, No Child Left Behind in 2002, and the Every Student Succeeds Act (ESSA) in 2015, more provisions were made to emphasize accountability and action for schools and students. This act focused on equity in the preparation of career and college readiness of all students, with a focus on marginalized and underprivileged youth taught and assessed through rigorous academic standards (U.S. Department of Education, n.d.).

Shifting Populations in American Schools

Since the turn of the twenty-first century, the racial distribution of children in U.S. schools has evolved, making some populations larger than others. According to de Brey et al. (2019), the racial distribution of school-age children between the ages of five and seventeen changed between 2000 and 2017, with White children at 51 percent in 2017, compared to 62 percent in 2000. In the same time frame, the percentage of Blacks decreased to 14 percent in 2017, down slightly from 15 percent in 2000.

However, other groups increased, with Hispanics growing from 16 percent in 2000 to 25 percent in 2017 and Asians from 3 percent to 5 percent. American Indian and Pacific Islanders changed by less than 1 percent. This change is evidenced in figure 5.1, which depicts the shift of race and ethnicity between 2000 and 2017.

Shifting populations, coupled with a rise in immigration, has directly impacted the dynamics of classroom management and the educational experiences for all students. Some teachers may find themselves underprepared to meet the needs of culturally and linguistically diverse students due to their own expectations of societal or cultural norms in the classroom.

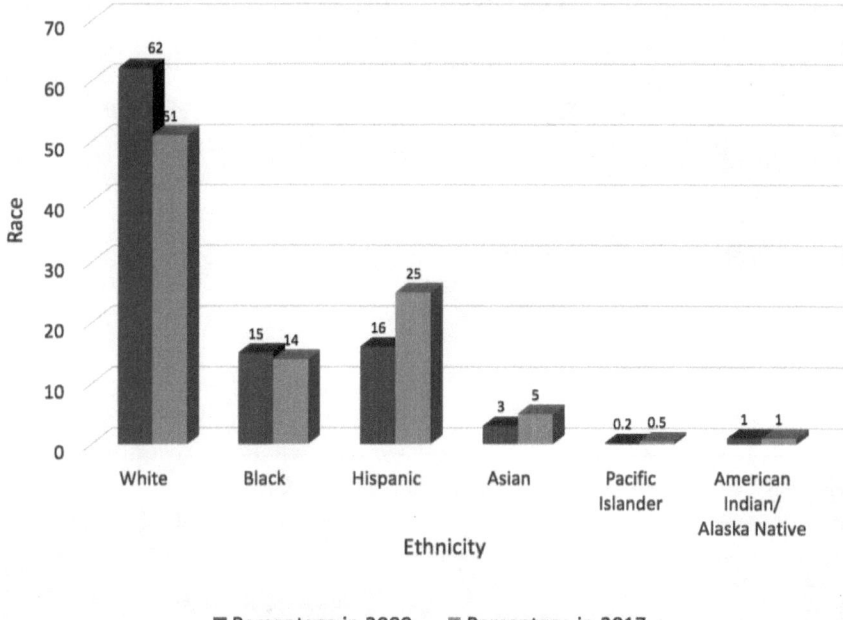

Figure 5.1 Race and ethnicity change in the United States from 2000 to 2017.
Source: de Brey et al. (2019).

Teachers' expectations of societal or cultural norms directly impact the rates at which culturally and linguistically diverse students are referred, identified, or classified as needing special services. These personal expectations can also impact the implementation of behavior plans or disciplinary actions because teachers may misread student actions, interactions, and overall work. To mitigate this, classroom teachers should reflect on their own implicit biases and values to have a clearer understanding of how these implicit biases influence both their expectations and interactions with students.

Figure 5.2 depicts the population of English-language learners (ELLs)—more recently identified as multilingual learners (MLLs)—throughout the United States in 2000. The largest populations of ELLs/MLLs were more prevalent in America's Southwest and West Coast, with state populations ranging, on average, from 7 percent to 23 percent in eighteen states. This is visually represented by the darker-shaded areas on the map. Seven states have between 4 percent and 6.9 percent, and the remaining states have between 0 percent and 3.9 percent.

The population of ELLs/MLLs throughout the United States in 2016 is depicted in figure 5.3. The ELL/MLL population shifts throughout the United States range from 7 percent to 20 percent in twenty states. Fourteen

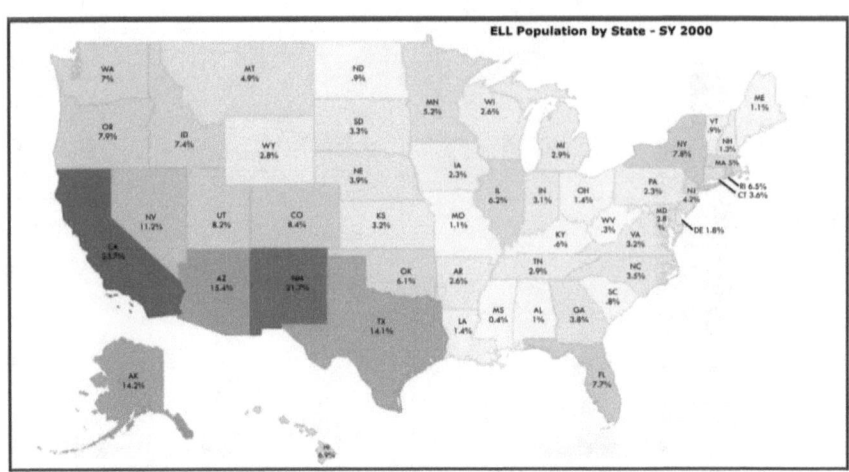

Figure 5.2 English-language learner populations by state, 2000.
Source: McFarland et al. (2019).

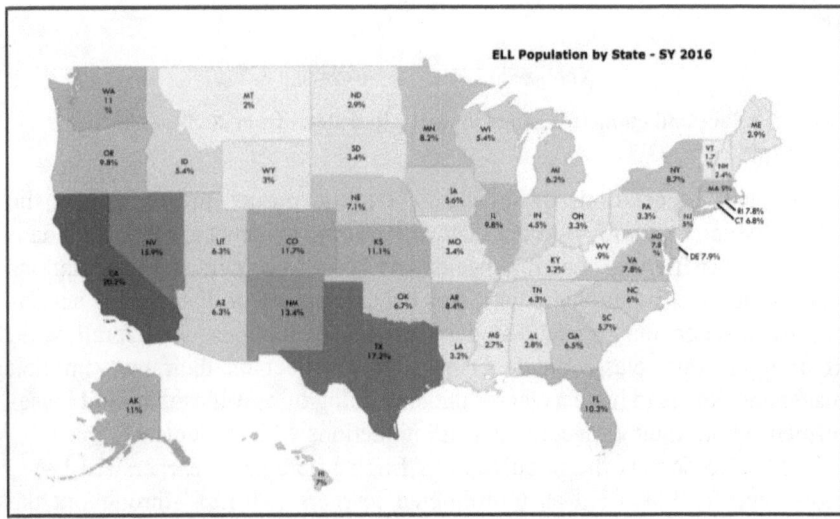

Figure 5.3 English-language learner populations by state, 2016.
Source: McFarland et al. (2019).

states have between 4 percent and 6.9 percent, and the remaining states have between 0 percent and 3.9 percent.

Comparing figures 5.2 and 5.3, the states ranging between 4 percent and 6.9 percent have doubled in number. The darker shades between the two figures indicate the shifting populations and how they have moved further north and east in the time frame of approximately fifteen years. According to the U.S. Department of Education (2018), an average of 14 percent of total public school enrollment was comprised of ELLs/MLLs in cities and 9.3 percent in suburbs. The predominant home language of MLLs is Spanish (76.6%), followed by Arabic (2.6%), and Chinese (2.1%).

What Do These Data Mean for Teaching and Learning?

To develop strong relationships that impact student success, it is essential to provide pedagogically and culturally sound instructional methods that affirm, value, and use cultural identities to embrace the uniqueness of students' backgrounds, histories, traditions, and practices. According to Leitão and Waugh (2007), "Positive teacher–student relationships are characterized by mutual acceptance, understanding, warmth, closeness, trust, respect, care, and cooperation" (p. 3). Building relationships and showing care is critical to student success. This is fundamental to classroom practice and is often the first opportunity for teachers to build a safe and welcoming environment for all learners.

Cultural competence is the ability for people to learn from, communicate with, and empathize with diverse groups of people to better understand and engage with those around them. Building these relationships helps students feel a sense of belonging and strengthen their self-esteem because they become receptive to learning and feel empowered to take risks.

According to Finley (2014), individuals may have different viewpoints or approaches to solving problems. Those lacking cultural competence may not understand or relate to how something is handled and deem responses as inaccurate ways to handle a situation, although it does make sense for the person (student, teacher, administrator, etc.) based on his or her background or culture. Culture is a "critical component of education" (p. 16), which should be viewed as an asset, not an extension, to the everyday classroom experience such as an activity incorporating a topic such as Martin Luther King Jr. Day or Cinco de Mayo in the classroom (New York State Department of Education, 2019).

The creation and implementation of meaningful curriculum and instructional practices lead to effective teaching and learning (Bransford et al., 2005) through asset-based approaches to build capacity or improve the abilities and skills of educators to benefit students. Educators can evaluate their approaches to engage, motivate, and interact with students by self-reflecting on the following questions:

- How do you use language (verbal vs. nonverbal) in the classroom to give instructions and explain student work?

- How do you express expectations for students, and how will they meet these expectations? What are your considerations in developing expectations for students?
- How do you focus on a positive learning environment with a growth mindset for all your learners? Is it your growth mindset, or is it based on individual students and their ideas and abilities?
- How often do you use different types of language, including colloquial speech, idioms, sarcasm, active/passive voice, etc., in your discussions with students? How does this impact student involvement and responses?
- How do you set students up for success? What does success mean for you and your individual learners?
- What learning tools do you teach students so that you can gradually release the learning responsibilities to them?

After responding to these questions, educators can consider the following suggestions for practice in the classroom, as listed in table 5.1:

The New York State Education Department is leading the movement to help schools and teachers provide welcoming and sustainable environments where children of various cultural identities can thrive. In 2019, it developed the Culturally Responsive-Sustaining Education Framework in response to many comments by the public, including school personnel, students, families, and stakeholders about ESSA and to provide a vision for education systems to embrace and explore access, participation, and learning outcomes for all students (New York State Department of Education, 2019).

Their work directly correlates to and is grounded in the work of Gloria Ladson-Billings' (1995) culturally relevant pedagogy. This vision provides stakeholders with an overview to co-construct and co-facilitate culturally relevant practices, with accountability measures for both short-term and long-term goals. Educators are expected to grow their ability to be sociopolitically conscious and socioculturally responsive. Four components are contained in the CR-S framework (New York State Department of Education, 2019):

- A Positive and Safe Learning Environment: This is a safe space where cultural identities are accepted, embraced, and "people are treated with respect and dignity" (p. 14).
- Challenging Instruction Supported by High Expectations: This considers the academically rigorous learning process and how learners are intellectually challenged to become independent risk-takers empowered to succeed.
- Instruction; Curriculum and Assessment for Culturally and Linguistically Diverse Students: Provides opportunities to "elevate historically marginalized voices" (p. 15), help people learn about perspectives beyond their

Table 5.1. Self-reflection and suggestions for practice in culturally and linguistically diverse classrooms.

Self-Reflection Questions	Suggestions for Practice
How do you use language (spoken and nonverbal) in the classroom to give instructions and explain student work?	• Provide written instructions for students to follow along. • Give students the opportunity to reword verbal instructions in their own way to give the rest of the class an opportunity to view it through the lens of their peers. • Understand the cultures of the students and professionals in the classroom. What hand are you using to hand out papers? What colors are you using for instruction? Are you using intonation or specific speech patterns? These nuances of how teachers unintentionally act may adversely impact student involvement and participation. Know your students.
How do you express expectations for students, and how will they meet them? What are your considerations in developing expectations for students?	• Present expectations through teacher-led discussion, on paper, and visually giving multiple opportunities for students to make meaning. • Allow time for students to comprehend expectations by discussing them with peers and journaling about it. • Provide student choice and/or input when considering expectations.
How do you focus on a positive learning environment with a growth mindset for all your learners? Is it your growth mindset, or is it based on individual students and their ideas and abilities?	• Have a clear understanding of what a positive learning environment means to you. • Provide opportunities for students to discuss and journal about positive learning environments. What have they experienced, or what would they like to experience within the learning environment? • Give students an opportunity to identify, develop, and understand their thoughts and ideas and abilities creatively.
How often do you use different types of language, including colloquial speech, idioms, sarcasm, active/passive voice, etc., in your discussions with students? How does this impact student involvement and responses?	• Colloquial speech, idioms, and sarcasm are often culturally specific. Things that make sense to you may have no real place in the classroom. They may be culturally irrelevant or condescending. • If you use this type of speech in the class, use it as teachable moments so students have an opportunity to make meaning from these speech patterns. • Honor the process and be open to learning from your students. It is not a one-sided engagement.
How do you set students up for success? What does success mean for you and your individual learners?	• Our idea(s) of success may not mirror that of students. Encourage students to be what they consider successful. • Provide opportunities for students to understand and visualize success in their own environment and culture. • Value the process.

What learning tools do you teach students so that you can gradually release learning responsibilities to them?	• Provide opportunities for students to engage and grapple with new and difficult information. • Give students time to process information to make sense of it through their own lens. • Honor the process daily and help students make meaning over time.

Source: McDermott (2020).

own understanding and knowledge, and dismantle fundamental ideologies of the systems of biases and inequalities in education.
- Ongoing Professional Learning Communities: Allow for the elasticity of teaching and learning for educators to grow and change through self-directed reflection.

These four components are foundational to the instruction and management of diverse classroom-learning communities. To examine and strip apart historical and culture-based ideologies, biases, and inequities, we need to engage students in culturally appropriate and responsive ways to explore both the past and present, to self-reflect, and to be responsive to difficult conversations, and delve into these concepts.

This process will assist stakeholders in navigating what they hear and experience in the street, at home, and throughout the school community (school, sports, intramurals, classrooms, etc.). Teacher awareness of diversity and the multiplicity of students and their cultures shed insight into the learning environment, learning process, and the effects that expectations have on student responses (Gabriel et al., 2011).

It is important to consider all stakeholders throughout the process, including students, teachers, school leaders, district leaders, community members, education department policy members, higher education faculty, and families when addressing the four components of the CR-S framework (New York State Department of Education, 2019). Table 5.2 represents an overview of the components and elements of this framework.

CONCLUSION

Acknowledging and embracing diversity properly in classrooms is complicated. According to Marzano et al. (2003), effective classroom management is the conduit for successful instruction and learning. The authors posited that "research tells us that the teacher is probably the single most important factor affecting student achievement" (p. 1). Furthermore, it is incumbent upon educators to establish environments where students feel supported and respected.

Table 5.2. The components and elements of the culturally responsive sustaining framework.

Components	Elements
Positive and Safe Learning Environment	• Collective responsibility to learn about student cultures and communities • Strengthening relationships • Embedding social-emotional learning programs • Providing materials representing student identities
Challenging Instruction Supported by High Expectations	• Opportunities for student leadership and civic engagement • Exploration of social justice through varied learning opportunities • Examination and rationale of power structures
Instruction, Curriculum, and Assessment for Culturally and Linguistically Diverse Students	• Inclusivity, design, and voice of all students in instruction, curriculum, and assessment • Varied resources with multiple diverse perspectives • Differentiated instructional strategies to meet the needs of all students
Ongoing Profession Learning Communities	• Training for inclusivity, with the examination of implicit and existing biases • Support for all voices of culturally and linguistically diverse students • Stakeholder inclusion in the process and direction of alignment

NYSED (2019). Culturally responsive-sustaining education framework. Retrieved from http://www.nysed.gov/crs/framework.

These factors, along with conscious and deliberate management strategies that uphold these ideas, lead to positive academic outcomes.

The changing student demographics in the United States may raise some challenges in the arena of classroom management because many teachers, administrators, and other stakeholders lack experience and training to address the cultural diversity of student populations in schools. Teaching should be a self-reflective practice in which educators take the time to consider their craft of teaching as it relates to the uniqueness of students.

Educators may also explore the suggestions for practice, highlighted in this chapter, to consider their own actions in valuing students. Furthermore, individual states and school systems within them should consider the guiding elements and components of the CR-S framework as they work together to address the uniqueness of individual students within a twenty-first-century school system.

REFERENCES

Asia Society. (2019). *Asian Americans then and now: Linking past to present.* Retrieved from https://asiasociety.org/education/asian-americans-then-and-now

Bernard, S. C., & Mondale, S. (2001). The educated citizen. In S. Mondale & S. B. Patton (Eds.), *School: The story of American public education* (pp. 19–60). Beacon.

Bransford, J., Darling-Hammond, L., & LaPage, P. (2005). Introduction. In L. Darling-Hammond & J. Bransford (Eds.), *Preparing teachers for a changing world: What teachers should learn and be able to do* (pp. 1–39). John Wiley & Sons.

Brophy, J. (2011). Classroom management as socializing students into clearly articulated roles. *Journal of Classroom Interaction, 45*, 41–45.

Caruso, M. (2012). *When the sisters said farewell.* Rowman & Littlefield Education.

de Brey, C., Musu, L., McFarland, J., Wilkinson-Flicker, S., Diliberti, M., Zhang, A., Branstetter, C., & Wang, X. (2019). *Status and trends in the education of racial and ethnic groups 2018* (Report No. 2019–038). U.S. Department of Education, National Center for Education Statistics. Retrieved from https://nces.ed.gov/pubs2019/2019038.pdf

Finley, T. (2014, August 14). *Four things transformational teachers do.* Retrieved from https://www.edutopia.org/blog/big-things-transformational-teachers-do-todd-finley

Gabriel, E., Woolford-Hunt, C., & Matthews, L. (2011). Culturally relevant approaches to classroom management. *Journal of Adventist Education, 73*(3), 38–43.

Huerta, G. (2009). *Educational foundations: Diverse histories, diverse perspectives.* Houghton Mifflin.

Ladson-Billings, G. (1995). Toward a theory of culturally relevant pedagogy. *American Educational Research Journal, 32*(3), 465–91.

Leitão, N., & Waugh, R. (2007, November). *Students' views of teacher-student relationships in the primary school.* Paper presented at the 37th annual International Education Research Conference, Fremantle, Western Australia.

Martin, J., & Sugarman, J. (1993). *Models of classroom management* (2nd ed.). Temeron Books.

Marzano, R. J., Marzano, J. S., & Pickering, D. (2003). *Classroom management that works: Research-based strategies for every teacher.* Association for Supervision and Curriculum Development.

McDermott, C. (2020). *Cultural competence: Best practices for instruction.* Unpublished paper, Molloy College, NY.

McFarland, J., Hussar, B., Zhang, J., Wang, X., Wang, K., Hein, S., Diliberti, M., Forrest Cataldi, E., Bullock Mann, F., & Barmer, A. (2019). *The condition of education 2019* (Report No. 2019–144). U.S. Department of Education, National Center for Education Statistics.

New York State Department of Education. (2019). *Culturally Responsive-Sustaining Education Framework* (CR-S framework). Retrieved January 9, 2020, from http://www.nysed.gov/common/nysed/files/programs/crs/culturally-responsive-sustaining-education-framework.pdf

Ravitch, D. (2001). As American as public school: 1900–1950. In S. Mondale & S. B. Patton (Eds.), *School: The story of American public education* (pp. 63–70). Beacon.

Walch, T. (2003). *Parish school: American Catholic education from colonial times to the present*. National Catholic Education Association.

Winzer, M. A. (1993). *History of special education: From isolation to integration*. Gallaudet University Press.

U.S. Department of Education. (n.d.). *Every Student Succeeds Act (ESSA)*. Retrieved January 15, 2020, from https://www.ed.gov/essa?src=rn

Communication Strategies Supporting Students for Grade-Level Transitions

Youn-Joo Park

The start of each school year is marked by the high hopes of teachers who are excited to meet new students and witness their "aha" moments in learning. As months pass, though, that glimmer of anticipation is dimmed by pebbles of challenges that begin appearing in students' learning journies. Teachers encounter students who face multiple challenges, some who struggle due to cultural or linguistic differences, others who have been identified as needing special educational supports, and still others who have settled into poor academic habits. These scenarios play out in classrooms across the county and can dampen the enthusiasm of teaching. Educators are justified in worrying about their students' readiness for greater academic challenges. To counter these concerns, teachers might apply strategic communication skills to help restore the classroom as a site of more active learning and smooth out the transition to the next grade level.

Using communication strategies can offer numerous benefits in educational settings and in classroom management. During the past century, the idea of *communication strategies* originated in corporate, public relations, with the focus on framing messages optimally for marketing purposes so that clients or customers are persuaded to buy a product or service (Bernays, 1945/2013). This concept can translate well into the current philosophy of education; teachers employ communication skills to motivate and persuade students to value knowledge and to exhort their students to put forth their best efforts. In other words, teachers seek to encourage their students to "buy into" the idea that advanced learning is to their advantage.

This chapter argues that communication is at the heart of education and can help address the socio-emotional development of students as they face new demands in their educational journey. The transitions to higher-level learning require the dedication of teachers from all grade levels because students need careful guidance to become intrinsically motivated, independent learners. The following asset-based communication strategies can be seamlessly integrated into the existing curricula to enhance students' academic success. Large-scale, drastic changes are not needed; rather, a bit more attention might be paid to a smoother transition between grade levels or school levels, which would lead to good classroom management as a natural by-product.

COMMUNICATION AS A CLASSROOM MANAGEMENT TOOL

The best communication strategies are proactive rather than reactive. The smooth functioning of the classroom depends on a rapid but thoughtful response, which can be exhibited through intentional, advanced planning. Some strategies might not require deployment because they are created for exigencies. Nevertheless, it is wise to preempt possible crises because a reactive response has the potential to elicit cursory solutions that do not address students' struggles. The optimal situation is for teachers to anticipate the difficulties of advanced learning and instill confidence and resilience among students to overcome various challenges.

Classrooms can also operate more effectively when teachers institute specific measures to achieve objectives. A good communication strategy comprises incremental steps toward comprehension that will not frustrate learners. For example, if the goal is for students to learn the value of scientific experiments, this might be prefaced by a lesson on independent variables versus dependent variables. Or if the goal is to have students write a strong thesis statement for an essay, there must first be proficiency in writing sentences with the correct syntax. The plan must account for the preexistence of foundational knowledge and corresponding skills accumulated through past instruction. Detailed planning is integral to the success of any endeavor.

Communication strategies should be broad enough to be both systematic and flexible. This sense of duality allows for standardization that stipulates the boundaries of behavioral expectations for all students as well as personalization that accounts for students' topics of interest and their individual learning abilities. An effective communication strategy might entail outlining expectations and boundaries while encouraging creativity.

By delineating differences between standardization and personalization, teachers can implement equity in terms of rules that apply to everyone versus individual freedom for unique expression and interpretation. For students navigating school or academic culture, they can develop the procedural understanding of what requires compliance from them and what grants autonomy to them.

In particular, grade-level transitions benefit when effective communication strategies are used as a classroom management tool, because in many educational settings, there exists a disconnect in the preparation for students' transition. Rarely is there a formal pre-transition, mid-transition, and post-transition available to students; rather, they are expected to go with the flow as circumstances arise.

To be sure, primary-grade students lack the scope of experience to fully participate in decision-making, so the child's developmental level needs to be considered. However, if schools do not fully communicate information or help them emotionally prepare for the transition, students may sense an erosion of their agency or personal control, leaving them in the dark and negating their emotional needs.

Although students might appear to be flexible with changes, transitions can elicit extensive emotional responses. These reactions may range from the positive (e.g., excited, curious) to the negative (e.g., fearful, apathetic, disruptive), with the latter response potentially leading to behavioral issues in the classroom. In fact, classroom management is a conundrum that all teachers grapple with in their quest to minimize class disruptions and maximize student learning. Every situation is unique and is based on a constellation of factors. Individual students have different levels of motivation, abilities, and dispositions, which are interfaced with teachers who also have different teaching styles, subject matter expertise, and personal dispositions. Furthermore, the policies from school, district, state, and federal levels have impacts in teaching. The maelstrom of variables collides and has a veritable influence on classroom climate and student learning.

In this context, teachers and administrators play an essential role in the educational success of students, and this applies not just to the high school level where college enrollment is imminent but to the entire educational spectrum from kindergarten through twelfth grade (K–12). Communication strategies intersect well with academic goals when teachers are cognizant of students' social, emotional, and cognitive needs and address these in a way that propel the momentum in learning.

Often, the complexities of classroom management, coupled with teaching demands, lead K–12 teachers to focus on the immediate needs of the classroom because there are sufficient adventures and dilemmas each day. Developing a clear perspective in midst of this chaos requires more intentionality via planning. Communication strategies can help refocus on the bigger picture because the reality is that education is a continuum whereby skills are enhanced, knowledge is accumulated, and the challenges become more complex.

The K–12 trajectory is set up to advance students gradually from one level to another. Indeed, the learning in elementary school is a pipeline to middle school, then middle school provides preparation for high school, and finally high school launches the students to college or a job. These levels are interconnected, although the communication between the levels can be disjointed at times. Since teachers at the primary and secondary levels are at different locations and may not interact with one another frequently, they can possess different notions of expectations, and this might unintentionally result in inconsistent communication conveyed to students.

In addition, taking the time to involve students in anticipating and preparing for the next grade level is important to facilitate the transition from the present to the subsequent school year. To offer continuity between grade-level transitions in K–12, for example, Graff and Birkenstein-Graff (2009) suggested there should be a common thread across various academic disciplines through the agreement on one core concept. They proposed that teachers of all levels should strive toward implementing the theme of *argument* because that concept naturally encompasses statistical reasoning, interpretation, and ethics:

> Unless we can formulate a unitary, overarching meta-vision of what unites us across the academic world, we will continue to make the experience of schooling a hodge-podge experience of rupture and disjunction for most students. (Graff & Birkenstein-Graff, 2009, p. W411)

The lack of continuity between grade-level transitions can have deleterious effects on student learning.

The primary education levels are certainly not alone in confronting this issue. Most studies on transitions have focused on college preparation at the high school level, and researchers have observed a huge communication disconnect between high schools and colleges (Conley, 2005; Venezia & Jaeger, 2013; Williams et al., 2018; Zimmerman, 1989). It is reasonable that high school teachers would focus on the present because they are in a high-pressure, time-limited environment with tons of content to cover.

However, the crack in the educational foundation becomes evident in postsecondary education. College faculty and librarians encounter patterns of academic struggles among students. This leaves them wondering whether or not the essential content was taught in K–12 schools. Are students unable to retain previously taught knowledge and skills, or is there truly a disconnect between what is taught at the secondary level and the reality of expectations at college (Saunders et al., 2017)?

If K–12 teachers wish to prepare students to surmount the challenges of higher-level learning, they must help ignite small behavioral changes among students to take ownership of their learning early on. These behavioral changes may include effective time management so that students reserve ample time to reflect on ideas and do their best work. Teachers can hone students' organizational skills such as keeping track of routines and submission deadlines that can earn them full credit for the completed work. Related to this organization is guiding students to pace themselves well in their assignments, so they can ask for clarity on a particular point or request assistance when needed.

The essential ingredient to learning success is showing up with an engaged attitude, and this "soft skill" can translate to other areas of life. It should be impressed upon students that no amount of academic knowledge can help them work up the motivation to successfully execute the work. College readiness skills go beyond simply content knowledge, and in fact, research emphasizes that behavioral and mental preparation for advanced learning is just as vital to academic success (Karp & Bork, 2014).

Based on this premise, a more effective way to prepare students for the expectations of advanced learning is for the preparation to begin at the primary school levels. Especially given that habits are long-lasting and are set early in life, elementary and middle school teachers have a major role in guiding students toward success in the later school years. Even the transition between grades at the elementary school level should not be overlooked because young students need validation of success and positive experiences in the classroom to cultivate curiosity and a thirst for learning.

At the middle school level, college readiness was addressed by teachers Burkins et al. (2016) in a published unit designed for their language arts classes. Activities in this unit directed students to consider their innate abilities and link those interests to possible job choices. This led students to expand their repertoire of academic skills such as browsing the library for relevant literature, obtaining a guided reading selection from the teacher, and then conducting independent research. The project had the benefit of allowing teachers to customize their instruction and for students to learn organically by utilizing their passions:

> We find that middle school, when students' quests for identity are on overdrive, is an optimal time to help students deeply explore the rich and diverse possibilities for futures that connect to the things that bring them joy. (p. 20)

Although the current K–12 educational system compels teachers to strive for better test results, Burkins et al. (2016) advocated that a project generated by the students' interests can help them develop agency and put them on the desired path, to not only a college major but a career of their dreams. This infusion of autonomy in the curriculum during the early school years can also foster intrinsic motivation, which is consonant with Ryan and Deci's (2000) motivation theories.

Priming students for success goes beyond the notion of academic readiness for more rigorous studies and instead incorporates the development of good habits, a positive mindset, and corresponding behavioral adjustments to realize the goals. These skills are perfectly teachable because they are "not personality traits or general cognitive abilities" but rather self-efficacy qualities like motivation, goal orientation, self-monitoring, and persistence (Conley & French, 2013). Other policy briefings echo these findings:

> Weak academic skills are not the primary source of poor course performance in Chicago schools. Students' academic behaviors (attendance and completing homework) are eight times more predictive of course failure than their test scores . . . Real improvements in learning will require states and districts to develop strategies that get students excited about learning, attending class regularly, and working hard in their courses. (Mazzeo et al., 2010, p. 26)

Enacting these behavioral patterns can pave the way to greater student engagement in learning and spur students to aim for goals they initially set for themselves.

An interesting aspect of success is that it can reinforce the positives for an individual. In self-efficacy theory, psychologist Albert Bandura (1997) said that people develop confidence through the mastery of a task because achievement can calibrate the proper understanding of their strengths. Therefore, applied to education, the gaps in student learning can be overcome when learners experience a modicum of success. The academic content gained in their formative school years position them to build upon that knowledge.

Teachers strive to create a positive learning environment to cultivate learning. The application of communication strategies offers a classroom-management technique to make the transitional process more transparent and organized for students. Ultimately, the idea centers on helping students develop good habits, so they can become lifelong learners and eventually make meaningful contributions in their career. The following discussion proposes five communication strategies that teachers can use to elevate learning to a higher level. The commitment from teachers of all grade levels is crucial to the success of this venture of incorporating effective communication in school transitions.

COMMUNICATION STRATEGIES

Within the framework of classroom management, teachers can utilize communication strategies before an unexpected complication arises. Although it is inevitable to avoid problematic scenarios in the classroom, it is possible to predict and prevent many complications. Perhaps the anticipation of complex academic challenges creates stress for learners, but the focus of communication strategies is to prioritize relationship building so that students feel safe to explore the new possibilities of the next grade level under the watchful and helpful guidance of the teacher.

The first communication strategy is to initiate dialogue. Teachers can reserve time to elicit students' concerns regarding the transition and intently listen to them. Once students' self-expression is acknowledged, then the second strategy is for the teachers to accentuate the positives. Students may express fears and anxieties, which the teacher can address by presenting information that corresponds to their concerns. The third strategy is to initiate some inquiry-based learning in the classroom, soliciting questions from students on what they are wondering about the next grade level. This activity can help students synthesize what they have already learned and reflect on what they wish to know so that the learning can be customized to topics of their interest. The fourth communication strategy is to present the rationale for the assignment. Clearly presented rationales enhance a student's ability to understand the purpose of the assignment. This practice also presents a student with opportunities to understand why intellectual challenges are helpful to them and how the completion of more challenging assignments will benefit them in their next stage of schooling. The fifth strategy is to form communication partnerships to reinforce the goals of a successful transition.

These strategies call for different levels of commitment from teachers in terms of resources such as time, energy, and logistics: "Easy lift" refers to activities that require lower levels of resources, whereas "heavy lift" refers to activities requiring higher levels of resources (see figure 6.1). Using even a couple of these strategies can make a difference in smoothing out transitions to the next grade level.

The following paragraphs further discuss the key aspects of communication presented in figure 6.1. Educators can implement these key aspects of communication to support their students during the transitional periods of their learning journey.

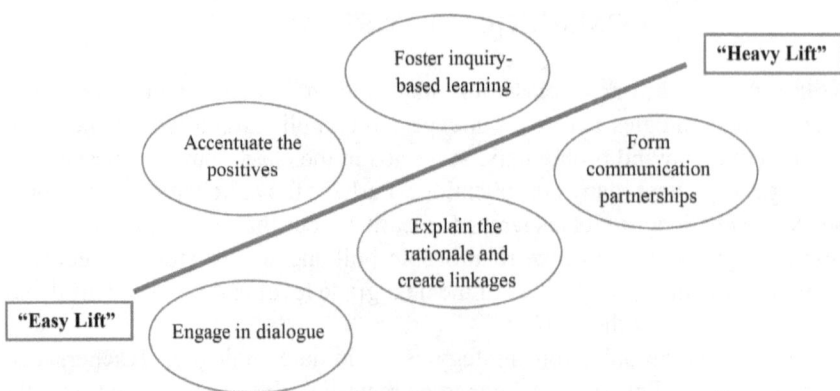

Figure 6.1 Resource Commitment Level of Communication Strategies.

Engage in Dialogue

In formal educational settings, the role of classroom teachers is communicating with their students via presentations, explanations, and class activities. The flow of talk has traditionally been from the teacher as the primary sender of messages to the students as recipients. However, some of the best learning takes place when the communication travels in both directions so that students can exercise some authority, or agency, over their knowledge-building process. Dialogue can be described as this bidirectional form of talk (Howe & Abedin, 2013), and it overcomes the limitations of strict hierarchy in the top-down model and replaces that with more horizontal, democratic interactions that can help share and expand knowledge.

By reflecting on the transitional concerns of students, teachers can incorporate personalized learning that takes into account students' interests and celebrates their abilities. The school year can begin with the teachers co-constructing the rules of engagement in the classroom while also getting to know the students' expectations and hopes for the class. Once the communication channel is opened to involve the contribution of students, then teachers may find classroom management to be easier because the dialogue is built upon the foundation of mutual trust and solution building.

The pedagogical advantages of dialogue are well documented in philosophy, which posits that exchanges of information help retain knowledge and increase empathy toward others (Bakhtin, 1981). Through talks, people can cultivate an open mind to new ideas, be awakened to different points of view, negotiate an agreeable solution, and make modifications as necessary. The idea of providing consideration and respect for ideas that contrast from one's own thoughts is essential to individuals' democratic role in civic society, and this notion of good citizenship can be practiced in the classroom.

Dialogue is also foundational in psychology to make sense of an individual's motives, emotions, and experiences (Vygotsky, 1978). Since good classroom management entails the reduction of disruptions to achieve a smooth learning process, the use of dialogue in the classroom can develop students' socio-emotional regulation regarding their reactions toward novelty. A transition may pose challenges on multiple levels, but when teachers retreat from the role of autocrat and encourage students to take the lead in voicing their thoughts, students can articulate their cognitive processes and emotions.

Deep listening by teachers can make the students feel heard and validated. The act of listening is an acknowledgment that students' emotions are important, so teachers can demonstrate respect for their individual reactions and thoughts. In essence, teachers become facilitators in this communicative process, because for there to be a resolution to problems, students need to first personally recognize these emotions and then learn how to express them.

When a teacher carves out time during the school day to elicit reactions to unfamiliar transitional demands, this action can confirm to students that their thoughts and emotions are perfectly valid. Once this is understood, then the conversation can move onto the next significant stage where the teacher supports the students' enthusiasm or addresses their concerns.

The active participation of students sharing emotions in the classroom helps with their self-regulation. This is not just an academic lesson but also a life lesson that has impacts on resilience. By setting aside time to engage in a conversation with students, the teacher conveys the idea that it is a worthwhile endeavor to process one's thoughts regarding a difficulty. As knowledge is expanded, fear can be minimized and excitement can increase, which are both positive results of dialogue.

In addition, relationship building can happen when the class atmosphere fosters understanding and support. As students share their reactions to the upcoming transition, they are likely to find other classmates who identify with similar emotions. Therefore, instead of feeling isolated and trapped in their own doubts and anxieties, students can feel comforted and develop solidarities from the conversation. This interaction has a positive spillover effect in the classroom through the creation of bonds and friendships among peers with whom they can share the emotions of being in the same journey. Once relationships have been established, then academic scaffolding can lead students to build upon their knowledge base by learning from one another (Vygotsky, 1978).

The listening role of the teacher is foundational in a healthy student-teacher relationship. The process of dialogue opens up the conversation so that teachers can avoid making assumptions about their students' feelings and knowledge gaps. Because teachers are naturally at a different stage of life than students, they may misinterpret students' reactions and emotions regarding the transition. When students communicate their concerns—and by extension, their current needs—teachers are enabled to personalize their teaching more. The dialogue can inspire teachers to incorporate the students' concerns into academic lessons such as a writing activity, an arts display, or a deeper challenge in sciences and math.

Although teachers are not transitioning along with their students, they can be instrumental in facilitating and preparing students for their next transitions through dialogue.

Accentuate the Positives

Transitions may lead students to display negative or lukewarm attitudes and behaviors toward changes, some of which are attributable to fears and anxieties surrounding uncertainties. However, these raw emotions can linger in the students' minds and manifest in negative ways not directly associated with a particular task. Teachers are often frontline witnesses to changes in student behavior through routine interactions, so they are in a good position to deploy a communication strategy that highlights the positives; doing this can effect changes in students' perspectives and, in turn, their behaviors.

The core tenet of progressive education is that achievement is possible through conscious improvement (Dewey, 1938; Ford et al., 2014). Based on this tenet, the identification and communication of uplifting messages are crucial to behavioral management because the genuine articulation of confidence and faith in an individual's abilities can result in the actualization of that belief.

In life, positive emotions can often be occluded by an overwhelming focus on negative emotions, and the situation is no different in a classroom. Students may not yet possess enough experience to put their concerns in proper perspective, so it might be useful for teachers to accentuate the positives. To alleviate students' anxieties, for example, teachers might frame the transition as indicating that they have outgrown their current stage and are ready to move on to higher-level learning. Talking about the challenge in this way encourages students to view the transition as a journey of personal growth.

Teachers might also model solution-based responses by articulating how some negative emotions can be transformed into favorable outcomes. There might be a class brainstorming session on the exciting features of the next grade level and a corresponding activity to organize these ideas by themes, so students can have the participatory experience of analyzing the benefits together. Cooperative learning on the topic of concern can allow students to contribute their ideas and thus actively engage in the reinforcement of a collaborative classroom culture.

Accentuating the positives can have multiple benefits for students, including cultivating a growth mindset for learning through planning, which emphasizes self-efficacy skills. The discussion on possible challenges and the formation of solutions as a group allows for analytical planning and the development of foresight, which both can result in the development of stronger academic skills. Not least, focusing on the positives can foster optimism and encourage a "can do" attitude so that students see the inherent value of perseverance.

Through class discussions, there can be mutual understanding of classroom behaviors that are valued. The practice of finding the positive in any situation puts into motion the skills that are important not only in the classroom but also throughout life.

Explain the Rationale and Create Linkages

To move the discussions on transitions from the conceptual level to the practical level, teachers can include some type of activity that helps identify what tangible actions constitute higher-level learning. Since the transition is on students' minds at the end of the school year, teachers can use this opportunity to communicate higher academic expectations to their students through class assignments.

The guidance that students receive in their foray into advanced learning, coupled with the comforts of the familiar classroom, translates into easier classroom management for teachers as they seek to introduce higher-level academic content and skill sets. For example, the simulation of the transitional expectations might serve as a trial event so that students can learn by making mistakes in a low-stakes setting where the result does not have huge negative impacts during the learning stage.

There can be enhanced student reception of complex content if teachers explain the rationale behind the work. Beyond giving details of the assignment, teachers can communicate the big-picture vision and articulate why the process matters in students' academic journeys. The explicit conveyance of a project's significance can help garner cooperation from students because they can more clearly understand the end goal and how these skills correspond to success in the coming years. When teachers draw connections between the rationale to the practical notion of what future challenges students may encounter, this can more easily gain the students' attention.

A broader approach to communication can help teachers create clear linkages for students who can then pursue their individual goals with greater confidence. This action is paramount, as large numbers of high school students are choosing to continue their education journey at the college level and a postsecondary degree is increasingly valued in the global workforce. For minority, first-generation college students, the challenge is not only enrolling in college but graduating as well (Nichols & Anthony, 2020).

One common problem observed by faculty in higher education is that students do not heed the parameters of an assignment despite having ample explanations. This occasionally results in documents written on a completely different topic or not addressing the major points. To prevent this issue from surfacing at higher grade levels, K–12 teachers can help students develop the habit of closely reading the content as well as understanding exactly what is being asked of them.

Like most forms of effective communication, the same message should be conveyed consistently across multiple methods. Teachers can verbally explain the assignment in depth, supplemented by a chart detailing the steps that students can follow. In addition, teachers can schedule individual "conferences" for students to monitor progress and to provide individual guidance where required. The practice can then be replicated in stages during class time while the teacher is present to help.

Even when a large project is completed under careful guidance in the classroom, there should be continued communication to drive the main point home. Rather than assume that students understand how to apply the academic strategies the next time, teachers should ask students what strategies they have applied in the most recent assignment that might help them work on similar projects in the future. By discussing successful learning strategies as an entire class, students who might have struggled initially are provided opportunities to learn from classmates. Highlighting the rationale of the coursework is crucial to inspire motivation among students—in fact, so important that the communication can be repeated at different occasions to reinforce the ideas.

To prepare students for higher-level learning, teachers should use class time to incubate the skills necessary for success, such as critical thinking, responsibility, and perseverance. By explaining why students should engage in learning, teachers can guide students to think creatively and logically to find solutions, hold them accountable for their work, and encourage them to continue trying beyond a few unproductive attempts. In the ever-growing quest to build students' knowledge and confidence, these are valuable skills that can last a lifetime. When teachers communicate the significance of learning, they connect challenging assignments to real-life values, thus expanding the applicability of the skills far beyond the classroom walls.

Foster Inquiry-Based Learning

Just as self-expression contributes to successful learning, asking questions is key to deep engagement with ideas. The types of queries that activate the greatest learning tend to probe what is not yet familiar. This creative form of inquiry facilitates knowledge because it requires more critical thinking than a question that seeks to simply confirm understanding or to obtain the procedural know-how of an activity. Thus, once the dialectical process is enacted, the teacher can sense the root of students' emotional response and solicit questions from students on what they wish to know.

An ironical circumstance of life is that curiosity comes naturally to young children who are fascinated by the world around them and cannot refrain from inquiring why something is, but as they grow older and settle into school routines, some stop asking questions and instead wait to be instructed on what to know. Therefore, the formation of questions can be difficult for students because the onus is on them to craft an inquiry rather than the habitual action of responding to a question posed by an authority figure.

Taking responsibility for one's own learning is not routinized. Thus, the challenge for teachers is to reignite that curiosity in their students and to transform the passive form of learning to an active one. An inquiry-based process requires students to figure out what they want to learn and to articulate it so that intellectual growth is embedded into their learning identity.

When starting to thinking about academic transitions, there needs to be relevant contextual information that provides sufficient background. Teachers can investigate the next grade-level differences and then present this information to students. One focus can be on class protocols. For example, a discussion on transitions can include differences in the structure of the day such as class duration, movement to different classrooms, the selection of courses, and general assignment expectations. After presenting these facts, the teacher can conduct brainstorming and discussions sessions, encouraging students to analyze the current schooling model and explore what elements differ from higher school levels.

Reflection may pose a challenge for elementary-grade students, but this is an essential first step, so they can engage in critical thinking about the upcoming transition and talk about plans to navigate the changes. The teacher can devote time for structured reflection by allowing the class several minutes of silent thinking and instructing students to come up with at least one question about the transition. If individuals seem to struggle with this initially, the activity could be assigned as a small-group activity. Either way, the objective is to create an environment of active learning so that students can take action (in this case, forming questions) based on the preliminary information they received.

When students consider the differences between the present situation and future possibilities, they can compare the scenarios and assume the primary role in preparing themselves by anticipating the impacts of the transitions. In essence, inquiry-based learning activities put students in the driver's seat.

In contrast to the dialogic process of responding to questions, students pose questions to the teacher, which represents the height of active learning. When students formulate and initiate the questions, they are intentional in their search for the answers and are more likely to retain the knowledge.

This inquiry-based learning also teaches skills useful to not only academic transitions but beyond, to future life scenarios. After all, substantive learning inquiries begin with wondering about a certain phenomenon and posing questions. Furthermore, teachers can lead students to a higher level of thinking, with eventual benefits to the learning dynamics in the classroom. When teachers focus on eliciting creativity and curiosity from students, the class can become engrossed in the communication activity, which creates fewer distractions from learning and fosters an improved learning environment overall.

Form Communication Partnerships

More than other strategies, this component of forming communication partnerships can involve a bevy of individuals who actively support their students' success. Communication does not have to remain the sole task of one teacher; messages of care and preparation get reinforced when individuals within the students' learning community get involved, such as other teachers, administrators, parents, and even older peers.

Generally, educators within a learning community focus on the success of their collective students. This shared commitment is most successful when they form teacher-to-teacher communication partnerships to ensure a smooth grade-level transition for all students. Every situation can pose fresh complications for effective classroom management and, at times, teachers may feel as if their classrooms are remote islands disconnected from others. However, through active collaboration, teachers can be assured that they are not facing the challenges alone. Logistics such as the time coordination of the teachers at different schools within a district can be difficult; however, the benefits of interactive, professional dialogue among educators are extensive when alleviating students' trepidations for an upcoming transition.

The creativity of the partnership is dependent on the unique teacher pairings, but one positive effect is that this arrangement can enhance classroom management through teachers' communication and support of one another. For example, an elementary school teacher might invite a middle school teacher to visit the classroom. This teacher of the next grade level could introduce himself or herself to the class, tell students what they might expect in the following year, and answer questions. The teachers can then together point out the differences in expectations between the grade levels, such as class policies, and provide a brief preview of the advanced content.

These conversation opportunities lead relationships to form before the grade-level transition and convey a sense of safety to students that the teachers at the next level are ready to welcome them. The bonus is that students get excited about a special event to meet a guest speaker who will likely be teaching them in the future.

In addition to building collaborative relationships among teachers, building and supporting collaborative relationships among students should also be encouraged. Not only might a teacher from the next grade level visit a classroom, but a group of older students might also visit a classroom and present their perspectives on transitioning. Upperclassmen can be assigned to meet with younger students to share their personal experiences and offer tips for a smooth academic transition. Research indicates that some older students desire a connection with their past school community ("I really wish we could have 1 day where we come back to year 6 to meet old friends and teachers") and that peer relationships are important among young learners (Ashton, 2008, p. 181). Facilitating connections that open communication channels can help all students aspire to higher education; for recent alumni, to take the leadership role of inspiring and mentoring younger peers also has its positive benefits. The potential benefits of these peer-to-peer interactions cannot be underestimated.

Administrators can also organize a site visit to the school for the upcoming class. This event gives students the opportunity to meet key people, including teachers and administrators. There could be classroom visits for students to see how classes operate differently from their current grade level. A tour of the spatial layout of the new school, including classrooms, science labs, the library media center, the gym, lockers, and the common student areas, can also lead students to look forward to the changes ahead. This partnership activity can dispel students' fear that they may get lost in the new school year and increase their confidence for the year ahead.

Another partnership that might be initiated is periodic communication between school district administrators and district graduates. School districts might routinely collect data from alumni through surveys and interviews to analyze the successes and setbacks in their academic trajectories (e.g., college and career), how their educational experiences helped them meet obstacles, and what can be improved (Massachusetts Education Equity Partnership, 2020). In this way, the information on transitions is not merely communicated at planned events during a student's time in-district but is also corroborated by long-range data regarding tangible results. This collected research would provide district administrators, school administrators, and teachers with relevant information through which to modify transitional preparations to improve the likelihood of students' success after middle school or high school. It would also confirm the importance of communication across the district.

Not least, the parents or guardians of the students play a critical part in the academic equation of success. The communication at home can reinforce good strategies for learning and personal development regarding transitional points (Education Services Australia, 2019). The added benefit is that parents can monitor the full range of a child's emotional responses to school transitions. Involving the parents or guardians in a transition partnership can help cultivate an effective communication exchange between the school and home. This practice would allow parents to closely follow updates from school and contribute to the academic transition efforts. Most significantly, this partnership can show a child that many people are committed to his or her well-being.

The logistical hurdles of forming communication partnerships are complex, because the process involves others outside the classroom. However, the challenges are negligible compared to students' enthusiasm that can be evident when partnerships convey future possibilities of higher-level learning and affirm the community's commitment to their success. Once students understand the roles they might play within a new environment, they can prepare for the transition with an optimistic attitude rather than react negatively to anticipated academic expectations or frustrations with unfamiliar challenges. This naturally leads to the smooth management of the class and a better learning environment because students are inspired to cultivate intrinsic motivation in their schooling.

All the participants in these partnerships can offer essential knowledge and guidance to children and adolescents, which in turn reduces the number of uncertainties and reinforces the skills students should develop in preparation for the transition. Although students might cling to the comfort of the present educational environment, the thoughtful application of communication strategies can help students develop the resolve needed to expand knowledge and hone the required skills for higher levels of learning. Carefully planned events would be conducive for students to not only dream but also muster up the courage to face the transition. Communication partnerships are truly vital to the actualization of student success.

COMMUNICATION AS PRAXIS

Grade-level transitions target student growth for higher-level learning, but signs of students' transformations and their academic readiness are subtle, because knowledge and skills are conveyed gradually over time, through the culmination of student-teacher interactions. In addition, the whirlwind of activities in each learning adventure makes this transition process difficult to pin down, given the diversity of students' learning needs. However, success in transitions are typically achieved "in the actual doing of it" (Garoni et al., 2021, p. 71). The transformative process, whereby theory becomes practice, is broadly known as *praxis* in the educational setting.

A critical juncture in students' academic journies is the advancement from the primary level to the secondary level, because the transition poses great unknowns for students who are accustomed to the old routines and the familiar social connections of their teacher and classmates. The earlier years of education are structured to introduce and practice behaviors required to do academic work. As students advance to the secondary level, they are expected to be more independent in their learning. This prepares them for college, where the workload, expectations, and complexity will become greater.

In this milieu, educators can use communication as praxis to highlight changes in learning expectations in advanced learning environments. Communication praxis strategies offer transformative experiences that support learners as they migrate from a tightly structured environment of K–12 grades to a more loosely structured environment of college (see figure 6.2).

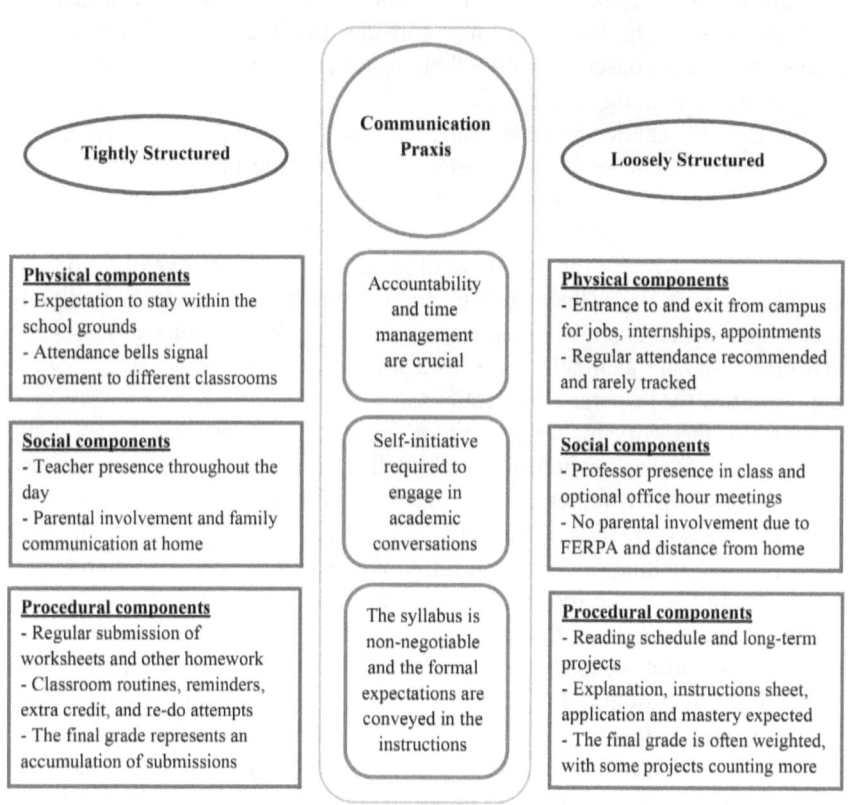

Figure 6.2 Communication Praxis in K–12 Versus College

These communication strategies are not overly specific, so there can be room for personalization. Establishing this understanding earlier in the academic journey means that students can prepare to become self-directed and develop confidence to navigate challenges.

As shown in figure 6.2, one reason it is difficult for students to transition from K–12 to college is inherent in the learning environment: the built-in accountability in the tightly structured environment of the primary and secondary school levels. To provide structure to young children, the school day is rigidly defined, with the expectation that students remain physically in the classroom unless the attendance bells dictate movement to another classroom. This physical constraint is suddenly loosened in college so that it might initially seem there is no structure (i.e., the student has officially become a manager of one's own time).

The expectation of self-management is clearly embedded in the autonomy of time management, and the praxis of accountability should be communicated repeatedly to students. A sudden amount of freedom can create the false illusion that there is little work to do, but this feeling can have disastrous consequences for students who may consider that the physical presence in a classroom is inconsequential to their learning or that other activities can supersede the learning schedule.

Another new challenge in the transfer of self-initiative from K–12 to college is that the teacher is not constantly in the same physical room as the student. Rather than have teacher presence throughout the day, the culture of college is that the professor is present during class instruction and reserves "office hour" visits for those who wish to discuss ideas or have questions on the materials. To the college student, there seems to be nobody immediately accessible, which creates a false sense of reality. The structure of college is that professors are available, only if the student would take advantage of the opportunities for in-person interactions.

Also in the college setting, there is no parent at the dinner table every night to check whether the child has completed the homework, so self-accountability is imperative to success in higher learning. Thus, teachers should impress upon their students the crucial step of taking initiative of one's education by seeking out assistance and conversations. This communication as praxis simulates the independence of adult life and instills the value that one must exert personal effort to achieve goals.

The procedural structure of work submissions is also different. K–12 students are accustomed to frequent verbal reminders and individual check-ups from their teachers who closely monitor and guide student progress. In college, that communication of built-in accountability is announced several times in class but then reinforced in written documents such as an instruction sheet. Therefore, the readings and deadlines are what students should heed on their own initiative through effective time management and their checkup of course materials.

College faculty often report incongruity between academic expectations and student expectations (Collier & Morgan, 2008). To overcome this gap, K–12 teachers and guidance counselors might take time to describe the college culture to students. Another practical instructional method would be to create a document that resembles a college syllabus to help students develop the habit of looking up the information on their own.

Grade allocations often differ in college, with a few projects counting more toward the final course grade, as opposed to K–12 levels where there is a frequency of smaller assignments that are cumulatively summed up for the final grade. Communicating this structural change and replicating it during the school year might help students anticipate the differences in assessments in higher learning where the stakes are higher. Given that working on long-term projects for several weeks is the hallmark of higher learning, it benefits students when certain classes simulate one or two of those types of long-term projects.

Since students will be migrating from a tightly structured to a more loosely structured learning environment, teachers can help by gradually loosening their direct supervision over the students' work. For example, teachers can assign a longer-term project that requires more individual effort from students, getting them accustomed to referring to a checklist or written instructions to maximize their autonomy over their learning. Students will likely encounter impasses and have questions while doing independent work, but plenty of encouragement and teacher presence at the K–12 levels can result in the development of strong academic habits.

Even if students become flustered, this presents a good opportunity for students to learn how to overcome hardships. It is important to teach students that failure is an opportunity to learn about one's innate talents and interests, so they should not take the setbacks personally or give up. In this way, the teacher communicates a broader applicable theory that self-motivation and genuine effort are just as important as academic content knowledge, for the content will vary from one field to another, but the skills for success will be fairly consistent across a diverse set of tasks.

Communication as praxis reinforces the idea of a larger scope of strategies that will maximize students' flexibility to apply the skills in whatever area might interest them. However, it is important that active engagement with learning communities is merged with the rigor of self-discipline to motivate and regulate one's progress. The right balance needs to be struck between collaboration and independence, and an earlier socialization to this concept would benefit students in K–12 classrooms. The praxis of change is ideally communicated through dialogue arising from both formal and informal social interactions within the classroom. By taking these steps, teachers can help students to prepare for a smooth transition between academic grade levels.

CONCLUSION

Communication strategies can successfully provide a bridge between the chasm of information and the lack of contextual experiences that are often present during grade-level transitions. Implementing these ideas can improve teachers' communication flow with students to illuminate major processes and allow anxieties and misconceptions to be addressed and dispelled. The pipeline of skills is developed throughout the school years, so the advantages will accrue over time.

This chapter focused mostly on pre-transitional communication because there are large disconnects to the subsequent grade levels. The following are communications strategies for teachers to bridge the gaps: (1) initiate dialogue, (2) accentuate the positives, (3) foster inquiry-based learning, (4) explain the rationale and create linkages, and (5) form communication partnerships. These strategies support teachers to prepare the minds and hearts of students for higher learning and enable them to carry out independently driven work.

A paradigmatic shift is not necessary to prepare students for higher-level learning. Rather, the ideas can be seamlessly integrated into existing curricula. Teachers can use these communication strategies to develop and cultivate students' academic strengths while taking into consideration both the developmental stages and the diversity of their students. For example, the focus for early elementary students could be on learning how to listen and follow directions, whereas later elementary students might learn how to differentiate between major ideas and supporting reasons. The instruction in middle school can continue this trajectory by helping students develop agency and regulation of their learning in preparation for high school. Then, at the high school level, students can prepare to enter a new educational world of advanced reasoning and counterarguments within longer, complex projects.

College behavioral skills such as self-motivation and deep inquiry can often be simulated in the classroom through the creative design of assignments, and the communication of expectations can allow students to become better acquainted with college culture. One major complication is that teachers at the primary and secondary levels are currently bound by directives that focus the curriculum on standardized testing because their students' test results are tied to school quality rankings and individual teachers' performance. The result is that teachers end up "teaching to the test." However, educators hold the power to revolutionize students' readiness for advanced studies, and the use of effective communication strategies can help learners develop their unique intellectual compass.

Despite the myriad challenges, all educators play a significant role in thoughtfully guiding students to achieve the best possible success across a spectrum of educational experiences. The ultimate vision should be broad, as in preparing students for college learning and career success. One lofty goal of education is to form well-educated citizenry, so success is dependent on the valuable contributions from educators of all grade levels. Building and supporting students' habits of self-efficacy is crucial, because, after all, the learning journey begins when it can be done independently and be sustained by the passion that only the individual learner can offer.

REFERENCES

Ashton, R. (2008). Improving the transfer to secondary school: How every child's voice can matter. *Support for Learning, 23*(4), 176–82.

Bakhtin, M. (1981). *The dialogic imagination: Four essays*. University of Texas Press.

Bandura, A. (1997). *Self-efficacy: The exercise of control*. Freeman.

Bernays, E. (1945/2013). *Public relations*. University of Oklahoma Press.

Burkins, J., Yaris, K., & Hoffmann-Thompson, K. (2016). College and career readiness in middle school: From George Costanza to Oprah Winfrey. *Voices from the Middle, 24*(2), 19–24.

Collier, P. J., & Morgan, D. L. (2008). "Is that paper really due today?": Differences in first-generation and traditional college students' understandings of faculty expectations. *Higher Education, 55*, 425–46.

Conley, D. T. (2005). *College knowledge: What it takes students to succeed and what we can do to get them ready*. Jossey-Bass.

Conley, D. T., & French, E. M. (2013). Student ownership of learning as a key component of college readiness. *American Behavioral Scientist, 58*(8), 1018–34.

Dewey, J. (1938). *Experience and education*. Macmillan.

Education Services Australia. (2019). *Understanding key transition points during childhood and adolescence*. Retrieved from https://studentwellbeinghub.edu.au/media/9830/swh_parent_transition_points_accessible.pdf

Ford, B. A., Stuart, D. H., & Vakil, S. (2014). Culturally responsive teaching in the 21st century inclusive classroom. *Journal of the International Association of Special Education, 15*(2), 56–62.

Garoni, S., Edwards-Groves, C., & Davidson, C. (2021). The doubleness of transition: Investigating classroom talk practices in literacy lessons at the end of primary school and the beginning of secondary school. *Australian Journal of Language and Literacy, 44*(2), 62–75.

Graff, G., & Birkenstein-Graff, C. (2009). An immodest proposal for connecting high school and college. *College Composition and Communication, 61*(1), 409–16.

Howe, C., & Abedin, M. (2013). Classroom dialogue: A systematic review across four decades of research. *Cambridge Journal of Education, 43*(3), 325–56.

Karp, M. M., & Bork, R. H. (2014). *"They never told me what to expect, so I didn't know what to do": Defining and clarifying the role of a community college student.* Working Paper No. 47, Community College Research Center, Columbia University.

Massachusetts Education Equity Partnership. (2020). *Strengthening student transitions to college and the workforce.* Retrieved from https://masseduequity.org/strengthening-postsecondary-pathways/

Mazzeo, C., Allensworth, E., & Lee, V. (2010). College prep for all? What we've learned in Chicago. *Education Week, 29*(3), 25–26.

Nichols, A. H., & Anthony, M., Jr. (2020, March 5). *Graduation rates don't tell the full story: Racial gaps in college success are larger than we think.* Retrieved from https://edtrust.org/resource/graduation-rates-dont-tell-the-full-story-racial-gaps-in-college-success-are-larger-than-we-think/

Ryan, R. M., & Deci, E. L. (2000). Intrinsic and extrinsic motivations: Classic definitions and new directions. *Contemporary Educational Psychology, 25*(1), 54–67.

Saunders, L., Severyn, J., & Caron, J. (2017). Don't they teach that in high school? Examining the high school to college information literacy gap. *Library and Information Science Research, 39*, 276–83.

Venezia, A., & Jaeger, L. (2013). Transitions from high school to college. *Future of Children, 23*(1), 117–36.

Vygotsky, L. S. (1978). *Mind in society: The development of higher psychological processes.* Harvard University Press.

Williams, M. R., Tompkins, P., & Rogers, B. (2018). High school teachers' perceptions of developmental education. *Journal of Developmental Education, 41*(2), 2–11.

Zimmerman, B. J. (1989). A social cognitive view of self-regulated academic learning. *Journal of Educational Psychology, 81*(3), 329–39.

Fostering Social-Emotional Learning (SEL) for Classroom Management

Amandia Speakes-Lewis, Amy Meyers, and Carrie Sollin

In this chapter, the topic of student's social-emotional regulation will be addressed through the lens of mental health practitioners, with practical suggestions for teachers to nurture and support these students within the classroom and curriculum. Developmental approaches will be highlighted through a social justice perspective.

In recent years, the United States has witnessed high rates of school violence, school dropout, youth suicide, bullying, and other destructive behaviors (Durlak et al., 2011). Adverse behaviors have raised the percentages of students coming into the schools with diagnosed or undiagnosed mental disorders such as depression and anxiety, among others. In fact, one in five youth have a mental health condition, with half of these conditions developing by age fourteen (National Alliance on Mental Illness, 2020).

Overlooked, undiagnosed, and inadequately treated mental disorders significantly interfere with a student's ability to develop and learn. Since students spend much of their productive time in educational settings, schools provide a unique opportunity to identify and treat mental health conditions by supporting students' needs within the classroom setting. When students' social-emotional needs are not met for their age-appropriate level, teachers often will be able to spot trouble signs within the classroom. These signs are listed in table 7.1.

Although these signs may look different for different age groups, these behaviors may get more intense and students' ability to cope with everyday stressors will become more difficult over time if the symptoms are not addressed. Furthermore, students' maladaptive behaviors can be much harder

Table 7.1. Emotional signs.

❑ Feeling sad or withdrawn	❑ Risk taking, impulsivity, or out-of-control behaviors	❑ Poor hygiene
❑ Crying regularly	❑ Drastic changes in behaviors or severe mood swings	❑ High anxiety or panic attacks
❑ Lack of motivation	❑ Difficulty concentrating or sitting still	❑ Eating or sleeping concerns
❑ Trying to harm self or others	❑ Substance use or abuse	❑ Social concerns or problems making friends or keeping them

Source: National Alliance on Mental Illness (2020).

to unlearn. Early intervention with concerns for students' social-emotional well-being is critical.

A key challenge for twenty-first-century schools involves serving culturally diverse students with varied abilities and motivations for learning, fueled by levels of emotional instability. Since classrooms have become an inclusive environment in the early 2000s, students' social-emotional regulation has been a topic of discussion across school districts. Regardless of whether students are working above or below the typical academic level for their age, they are placed in classrooms with their chronological age mates rather than considering the differential needs of students of diverse backgrounds.

As more children with physical, intellectual, and emotional regulation issues are included in the "regular" classroom, teachers have to discover new ways to be able to meet the needs of all students within their classroom through a Universal Design for Learning method. Classroom teachers are required to meet the academic needs of every student, while simultaneously identifying and intervening in their social-emotional issues. The unfortunate consequence is that students who lack social-emotional competencies often become less engaged, which leads to diminished academic performance and behavioral issues (Blum & Libbey, 2004).

Educators continue to debate and determine best practices to support students with social-emotional dysregulation. The benefits and challenges of inclusive classrooms continue to emerge and challenge the educational system. Although progress has been made, much more is needed to support incoming generations of students.

ETIOLOGY OF SOCIAL-EMOTIONAL DEVELOPMENT

A child's education begins at birth when an infant observes and mimics others. As for a young child, more formal ways of learning occur through the introduction of preschool experiences or through playdates with other young children. The shaping environment includes caregivers, siblings, peers, and educators. Once elementary school begins, academic lessons become the focus of education, and this continues into adulthood. But even then, education is much more than simply gaining knowledge; it is about growing a sense of self through personal and interpersonal stages of development. Children's social and emotional experiences influence brain development, which is central to outcomes in learning, behavior, and health.

Many factors may cause a student in a classroom to present with social-emotional dysregulation. Some children may be biologically predisposed to social-emotional dysregulation and may have difficulty in a structured learning environment around peers with varying abilities. Research supports the fact that a child's environment can be responsible and that some home environments may not foster the developmental needs of a young child (Durlak et al., 2011). This validates the idea that caregivers who do not model appropriate behavior in managing day-to-day stressors could lead to a child's social-emotional dysregulation, which may present in a school setting as behavioral issues.

Behavioral Indicators

From early childhood to adolescence, the lack of behavior control in the classroom is typically the first indicator of social-emotional dysregulation. Table 7.2 shows behaviors that may indicate a lack of social-emotional competency.

To foster students both academically and social-emotionally, teachers need to identify and address these maladaptive behaviors. Depending on the students' age or development, they may be unable to ask for help or have not learned how to cope with everyday stressors, so their need for assistance may be shown through disruptive behaviors within the classroom.

Table 7.2. Behavioral indicators.

❏ Ignoring the teacher's directions	❏ Refusing to share or cooperate with others and arguing continually	❏ Whining, crying, or throwing temper tantrums when required to acquiesce
❏ Using delaying tactics	❏ Demanding immediate gratification	❏ Verbally abusing or bullying others
❏ Resisting following directions	❏ Calling out answers	❏ Taking things from others
❏ Trying to get others to do their work for them through manipulation	❏ Trying to manipulate teachers	❏ Pushing ahead in line

Source: Nye et al. (2016).

Since this book focuses more on classroom interventions, the authors will not discuss further what can be done within the home or community environment to foster social-emotional learning (SEL); yet it must be acknowledged that the family, school, and community must work together to support student development. It will take more than one environment to nurture our students' social-emotional development. Society, families, and educators can assist students with their social-emotional regulation by exposing them to experiences that will reshape their motivations, awareness, and responsibility. Therefore, it is one responsibility of educators to assist students struggling with self-regulation skills.

School Community as Agents of Change

In recent years, the educational landscape has shifted to reflect a growing emphasis on SEL in K–12 schools. We are seeing strengthened efforts directed toward educating the "whole child," which includes both academic and nonacademic areas. Teachers strive to provide their students with more dynamic and comprehensive learning experiences. Both educational and psychological research indicate that a child's ability to maintain healthy relationships, carry on a productive and respectful conversation, make responsible decisions, and empathize with others all influence that child's ability to succeed in academics (Darling-Hammond et al., 2019).

One strategy to support social-emotional growth for students includes creating a clear system of expectations, not only in the classroom but also within the entire school environment. Students learn social-emotional well-being through collaboration with their teachers, peer-to-peer exposure, and with encouragement from their families, rather than on their own (Durlak et al., 2011). Emotions can get in the way of student learning and success in school. Self-regulation is a critical skill to learn, especially at a young age. Thus, school-wide consistency is key to classroom management, as it will foster social-emotional growth in and out of the classroom setting (Nye et al., 2016).

Research that dates back to the late 1990s has supported the idea that integrating emotional expression in a caring classroom atmosphere improves memory and stimulates the brain to learn and retain information (Green, 1999). Current brain research supports the idea of the mind-body connection in terms of bringing students to a higher level of learning when the mind and body are nurtured. Because of this research, SEL is now being incorporated into the curriculum.

In the past decade, it has been theorized that universal school-based efforts to promote students' SEL represent a promising approach to enhance children's personal growth and academic success (Durlak et al., 2011). Taylor et al. (2017) have argued that working with students through SEL has been shown to improve positive youth development skills such as self-control, interpersonal skills, problem solving, quality of peer and adult relationships, and engagement in academics.

FOSTERING SEL

Social-emotional learning is defined as "the process through which children, youth, and adults acquire and effectively apply the knowledge, attitudes, and skills necessary to understand and manage emotions, set and achieve positive goals, feel and show empathy for others, establish and maintain positive relationships, and make responsible decisions" (Collaborative for Academic, Social, and Emotional Learning, 2020, para.1).

In May 2018, the New York State Education Department Board of Regents permanently adopted proposed amendments to Sections 135.1 and 135.3 of the Commissioner's Regulations, Educational Law 804 (New York State Education Department, 2018), clarifying that all grades are required to include mental health and regulation of physical and mental health within their health programs designed to enhance student understanding, attitudes, and behaviors that promote health, well-being, and human dignity.

The change in legislation promoted the expectations that districts need to educate and foster the *whole* child, which means academically and developmentally. Many other states, besides New York, have recognized the importance of including SEL into the classroom curriculum, although these mandates vary state to state in its development and implementation.

Today's schools are increasingly multicultural and multilingual, with students from diverse social and economic backgrounds. Educators and community agencies serve students with different motivations for engaging in learning, for behaving positively, and for performing academically. Every child has the capacity to learn when exposed to effective and relevant learning strategies. SEL provides a foundation for safe and positive learning, and it enhances students' ability to succeed in school, careers, and life (Weissberg, 2016).

In a recent national survey of teachers, 95 percent of respondents said that SEL is teachable and 97 percent said that SEL can benefit students from all socioeconomic backgrounds (Bridgeland et al., 2014), making this addition to the curriculum key to student development and success. Implementation of SEL involves creating practices and policies that help students acquire and apply knowledge, skills, and attitudes that enhance personal development, social relationships, ethical behavior, and productive work in school. From providing explicit instruction on how to practice self-management to productively relating to peers and engaging in empathy, SEL is increasingly recognized as critical to every child's development.

As educators, we must also recognize the importance of crafting SEL initiatives at a district-wide scale and integrating SEL into academic instruction. Ideally, time spent on SEL throughout the school day should be meaningful, strategic, and research-based, but that is often easier said than done. SEL is still a growing field, and researchers are continually expanding and refining their understanding of pedagogical best practices as well as the role of educational technology in SEL. As researchers uncover more insights, the classroom momentum cannot be put on hold: district leaders, principals, and teachers are all learning in real time, through relationships with students in the classroom (Weissberg, 2016).

Research shows that SEL not only improves achievement by an average of 11 percentile points, but it also increases prosocial behaviors (such as kindness, sharing, and empathy), improves student attitudes toward school, and reduces depression and stress among students (Durlak et al., 2011). SEL interventions have also been shown to be effective in promoting targeted social and emotional competencies with short-term and long-term effects, which results in both enhanced social and academic adjustment and reduced levels of conduct problems and emotional distress (Durlak et al., 2011; Taylor et al., 2017; Weissberg, 2016).

It would be best for teachers to incorporate SEL programming into their curriculum in a universal manner to be able to meet the needs of all students within the classroom. Yet sometimes, a more targeted approach will be needed to foster students in greater need of developing their social-emotional regulation where growth is unsuccessful.

Students who may benefit from more selective SEL interventions may be a class of students, families, or communities with demographic characteristics and/or life experiences that place them at risk for late or poor development. Students within this group may be living in poverty or disadvantaged neighborhoods, be exposed to different levels of trauma, or have parents with mental health or substance abuse disorders (Weissberg, 2016).

Another group of students that may benefit from a more targeted SEL program are students who show early signs of difficulty with their social-emotional development. Often, these students receive a mental health diagnosis or a special educational classification. A comprehensive and collaborative team would be needed within the school community to support the students with more severe social-emotional needs.

One of the best ways that teachers can meet the social-emotional regulation of children is to help them develop the social and emotional skills they need to be resilient. Children who know how to cope with challenges, overcome obstacles, and adjust to changes in their lives often get along with others and develop other important social-emotional skills. Resilience is important for children because it gives them emotional stability in unknown situations and helps them develop skills necessary to be successful in life (Kaplan Early Learning, 2020).

It is so important to provide educators with actionable strategies, next steps, and examples to effectively work toward fostering these competencies in the classroom. Social and emotional learning is complicated, and every student enters the classroom with a unique set of SEL needs. Therefore, they often require an individualized approach to SEL practice and empowerment specific to their age level. In any area of education, a teacher's awareness of and relationships with students can serve as a powerful driver for delivering individualized or differentiated instruction.

FOSTERING POSITIVE SOCIAL-EMOTIONAL DEVELOPMENT IN THE CLASSROOM

Role of Educators in Fostering Classroom Behavior

At the core of SEL is the effort to help students manage their emotions, develop and display empathy, cultivate positive relationships, and achieve goals. The path toward the development of social-emotional skills begins with the relationship between students and teachers and is successfully navigated by the ways in which they interact.

Some parents have the notion that children will respond to punishment in the hope of reinforcing "good" behavior and discouraging the "bad." Teachers are also likely to use the reward/punishment system in an attempt to manage classroom behavior. However, punishments are particularly counterproductive in regard to positive social-emotional development. In fact, children's behavior improves when teachers relate to the students in a manner that is calm and consistently supportive, even in the face of challenging behavior. Social and emotional development is promoted by modeling, teaching skills, and allowing students to apply such skills (Jennings & Greenberg, 2009).

Promoting social and emotional development for all students in classrooms involves teaching and modeling social and emotional skills, providing opportunities for students to practice and hone those skills, and giving students an opportunity to apply these skills in various situations. It also requires having a growth mindset: the idea that individuals are capable of developing the skills or characteristics that may not be readily available or recognizable. People are capable of change, so it would certainly be wrong for educators to stigmatize or label those with challenges as "difficult" and act discriminatory.

If educators adopt the value that individuals can be open to learning through interactions, then educators are empowered to create change.

Too often, teachers underestimate their influence as authority figures. We may do this by being uncomfortable with our own authority and the "power" we wield in our role as teachers; by undermining our own ability to be able to "change" a student; or the luxury we may have to be a positive influence through relationships. We also tend to underestimate the power of listening. Most people have been listened to but may not have had the experience of truly being heard. Students with social-emotional challenges generally do not draw people toward them. With the growing responsibilities in the classroom and the lack of academic and paraprofessional support, it can feel like quite a burden when there is disruption. It becomes easy to lose empathy, to let bias creep in, and dismiss the disobedient student. However, if attention is paid and interest shown, the power of caring has immeasurable rewards.

There are several strategies that classroom teachers can adopt to provide a social-emotional framework in their classroom. First, it is important that the teacher's expectations for behavior are age appropriate. All of the strategies discussed below serve to build community, encourage reflection, develop self-esteem, and manage emotions. These are the cornerstones of academic and relational success.

Building Community through Empathy, Reflection, Communication, and Cooperation

It is imperative to foster a positive school environment and create an inclusive climate. Children thrive in an atmosphere of warmth, acceptance, and support. When students are in distress, listening is integral to help them feel better. When individuals feel good, they want to be with the person who provided those good feelings and they will likely do what is needed to maintain that positive relationship. Conveying empathy not only makes individuals feel metaphorically "held" but also allows them to develop empathy for others.

Empathy should be taught at home and in school. It is not something that must literally be a teaching point, though focusing on teachable moments makes this skill relevant. It is about conveying empathy to a child through interaction; it must be cultivated through modeling, relating, and responding. When children feel validated in their experience and feelings, they begin to mirror those emotions to others. In turn, those who experience empathy are able to then demonstrate empathy to others.

This is on par with social learning theory (Bandura, 1976), in which children learn behavior through observation, imitation, and modeling. In addition to modeling empathy, it is imperative that children are able to feel empathic, which requires the development of a moral conscience. It also requires the ability to perceive situations from multiple perspectives, rather than through one's own singular lens. Part of this comes with cognitive development, but it is also a result of SEL.

Strategies to Foster Empathy

Here are some specific strategies on how to incorporate empathy and encourage compassion in the teaching practice:

1. Develop perspective taking. It is incumbent upon adults to tend to children's perception of their experience, certainly when it comes to a school environment and creating a safe space. Validating a child's experience is the first path toward allowing that child to experience empathy. Therefore, when an incident occurs in the classroom, the first line of action should be to listen to the child. The "truth" of what has occurred is not as important as the child's perception of what occurred.

Since empathy requires taking in someone else's perception, the next step would be to ask the child how other student(s) involved might have experienced the situation. For example, rather than only making students apologize for their actions or behavior when they offend another, teachers can consider asking offending students how they think the offended student may feel by what is said; how would this child feel if someone else said the same thing to them? With these reflective questions, students are likely to develop the ability to put themselves in another's emotional place. But first, they have to be "fed" (or emotionally held) in order to feed another (Bowlby, 1969).

You can further help students develop compassion by asking them to think about the implications of their actions for the group. Direct them to imagine what would happen in various scenarios, as indicated in table 7.3.

The classroom environment is a rich space to cultivate cooperation, negotiation, and empathy.

A teacher can have a mission statement incorporating the following, as indicated in table 7.4. Develop this mission statement with your students.

What is required for students to feel safe? To feel accepted? To be liked? Table 7.5 provides examples of what teachers can do to encourage a safe environment.

2. Set expectations for behavior. Create ground rules in your classroom and do so by soliciting students to contribute their ideas for proper classroom etiquette. If in need of a teacher-student discussion, explain the practical reasons why it is necessary to share, take turns, raise one's hand, and be respectful. Convey that while there will be consequences for continuous inability to abide by rules, do not make that the motivation for behavior.

Table 7.3. Compassion scenarios.

What Would Happen If:
• Everyone called out whenever they wanted to. • No one cleaned up or put things back where others could find them. • You had been waiting 10 minutes and someone cut in line ahead of you. • The school library had no books for you to do your report because someone had taken more than needed. • Someone called out the correct answer to a difficult question when it was your turn, and you knew the answer. • No one chose you for the team during recess.

Source: Jennings & Greenberg (2009).

Rather, explain that the issue is not about following or not following the rules but rather how their actions might affect others. This is instrumental in developing compassion and empathy. It is important for students to know and understand why the rules and procedures established for the class are necessary, not arbitrary, and why acceptable alternative ways of behavior are more appropriate than undesirable ones.

3. Cultivate diverse perspectives. It is also important to cultivate empathy for diverse individuals. The more diversity in your life, the better able you are to also model this attribute. Just like it is hard to cultivate empathy in another if we are not empathic, it is hard to expect a certain behavior to be learned without parallel modeling. We grow from exposing ourselves to new experiences and to people who look different than us. We are living in a culture where we are drawn to sameness (Tatum, 1997). Oftentimes, differences breed discomfort, if not contempt. It is important to capitalize on the diverse student representation within a classroom. Solicit the sharing of experiences both outside and within the classroom. If there is not diverse representation, consider ways to integrate diversity and the development of cultural humility (Rivera, 2020). What is the school's mission around diversity and inclusion? What efforts are undertaken to create an atmosphere of acceptance? How is the teacher creating an inclusive learning environment? Table 7.6 provides examples of culturally responsive ways to create an inclusive learning environment.

Table 7.4. Mission statements.

Have a classroom mission statement incorporating:
What are the expectations of the classroom climate? What will be the culture of the classroom?

Source: Schiering (2017)

Table 7.5. What teachers can do to encourage a safe environment.

What Teachers Can Do...

❑ Acknowledge acts of kindness, establishing it as a norm.
❑ Develop a curriculum that addresses the value of acceptance.
❑ Provide opportunities to talk about feelings.
❑ Based on any lesson, ask students how they would feel if they were that person you are educating them about.
❑ Display posters with feelings options; ask students to identify their feeling state;
    This can be elaborated on by inquiring what is making them feel that way.
    This can progress to asking students how they think another student may be feeling based on their facial expression or mood.

4. Facilitate compassion and social awareness. Compassion is another aspect of empathy development. For example, students with social-emotional issues can visit programs that provide services to others and facilitate interactions with people of various backgrounds. They may also build connections, find support, and build community through service-learning projects, which also lead to mentorship opportunities.

Students can also talk with students who have been bullied, been exposed to ethnic or gender abuse, and so on, so they can learn what it feels like to be the victim of someone else's behavior and develop empathy. Offering them the chance to help others can also make them feel good about themselves. Social awareness is cultivated by understanding social norms, the array of different experiences, and bearing witness to the behavior of others.

5. Foster cooperative learning. Involve students in cooperative learning projects so that they understand how they can benefit from helping one another and working together. This method de-emphasizes competition. As part of the assignment, they can be asked to reflect on a few ways that they will gain knowledge, information, or skill from working with someone else and how they may contribute to the other student's knowledge, information, or skill building. Remind students often that others are more likely to help them if they help others. In theory, working together in small groups will give students enough satisfaction so that they will want to relate better to their peers. This also holds true with skills of cooperation, negotiating, managing conflict, and active listening, which are all pivotal to collaborative development. Not only do teamwork and group projects create opportunities for healthy relationships, but they also build communication skills.

6. Demonstrate caring behavior. Another technique for increasing the caring behavior of students is to act in a caring manner toward them. The role of a teacher to educate must become more broadly defined. Teachers play

Table 7.6. Examples of being culturally responsive.

Teachers can be culturally responsive by...

- ❑ **Being attuned to the diverse social emotional learning needs of students.** Students from vulnerable populations may be challenged socially and emotionally. When we consider the needs of diverse students, we must consider the variation in access to resources that may be imposed by learning disabilities or being a racial or ethnic minority.
- ❑ **Modeling interest and acceptance in all students regardless of race, gender, religions, disability, etc.** This requires accepting that we all have been socially constructed to see certain differences based on color, for instance, rather than based on verifiable biological attributes or differences (Tatum, 1997). It means we must see color rather than purport to be color blind. When we claim to be color blind, we are not acknowledging the structural racism that exists and we invalidate life experiences. Furthermore, we fail to acknowledge our own implicit biases. If we acknowledge these differences in life experiences due to race, then we can strive to create inclusivity and we draw out and celebrate these differences (Saphier, 2009) rather than simply tolerate them.

Source: Rivera (2020).

an important role in socializing and emotionally supporting students toward developing their sense of competence and self-esteem while training them to be good citizens (Schiering, 2017). Teachers can spend time with students doing things that the students choose, whether that is shooting baskets, drinking soda, or lending a sympathetic ear to what the students have to say.

Having informal time with students does not mean that boundaries are crossed. The quality of the relationship and the appropriate manner of relating is the key to modeling. One should not get bogged down in formality of situational context. During class, teachers can demonstrate their interest and concern for certain students by providing them with a little extra attention, writing more detailed comments on their work, and actively listening when the students voice their personal concerns.

The task of educators is to help students develop multiple perspectives, strengthen critical-thinking skills, and make sound decisions. Being flexible with ways of learning and teaching and finding creative ways for students to engage are critical.

ADDRESSING SOCIAL-EMOTIONAL CONCERNS IN THE CLASSROOM

As indicated earlier in the chapter, effective social and emotional learning involves the school community as a whole, with coordinated efforts within the classroom, the school, the district, the family, and the community to create policies and practices that help students develop five key skills. These skills include self-awareness, self-management, social awareness, relationship skills, and responsible decision-making skills (Collaborative for Academic, Social, and Emotional Learning, 2020).

- Self-Awareness—Identification of emotions, recognizing strengths, self-confidence, and accurate self-perception
- Self-Management—Impulse control, stress management, self-motivation, and organizational skills
- Social Awareness—Empathy, appreciating diversity, respect for others
- Relationship Skills—Communication, social engagement, relationship building, and teamwork
- Responsible Decision Making—Identifying problems, analyzing situations, evaluating and reflecting (Collaborative for Academic, Social, and Emotional Learning, 2020)

Addressing social-emotional skills at all levels of education is beneficial for developing and enhancing the skills addressed previously. These skills can foster SEL through a variety of educational approaches that promote students' capacity to integrate thinking, emotion, and behavior to deal effectively with everyday personal and social challenges within the classroom. The objectives of these skills that teachers can utilize in the classroom are to help students:

1. understand and manage emotions,
2. set and achieve positive goals,
3. feel and show caring and concern for others,
4. establish and maintain positive relationships, and
5. make responsible decisions.

Helping students to address the components of SEL through these above-mentioned skills is different based on the student's school level as described in table 7.7.

Elementary School

According to Zastrow et al. (2019), elementary education is a time to foster SEL by supporting children to acquire knowledge and values, etiquette, rules, behavior, social expectations, and information necessary to get along with others and thrive in a school setting. Children learn to interact with other people and understand which behaviors are considered acceptable and which are not. As a result, little by little, children adjust to the fact that they must control their behavior, work toward daily goals, and become more independent. Young children who have not learned this and who experience challenges in meeting these expectations need support with developing social-emotional regulation.

The following vignette provides a profile of an elementary school-age student who is experiencing some social-emotional challenges and what may be seen in the classroom setting.

Vignette

> Kevin is a seven-year-old second grader who has an Individualized Educational Plan (IEP) because of behavioral concerns identified in the classroom. It was noted in Kevin's IEP that there were also some behavior issues in his previous public school. In first grade, he was described as "unruly," "stubborn," and "lacking in social skills." His first-grade teacher reported that he had difficulty sharing and taking turns. He hit other children when they did not give him his way and often rebelled or had temper tantrums when his teacher reprimanded him or enforced the consequences that resulted from his challenging behavior.

Teacher's Classroom Observation in Addressing Social-Emotional Concerns

Because Kevin is a student with an IEP, there may be underlying challenges that impact his social-emotional skills in the inclusive classroom. Kevin requires a supportive environment that identifies and addresses the specific function of his noncompliant behavior and direct, explicit social skills training. Behaviors that might indicate delayed social-emotional regulation include the following:

a. Not following directions
b. Calling out in class
c. Refusing to share or cooperate with others
d. The inability to control emotions
e. The inability to make friends

Table 7.7. *Social-Emotional Learning Skills*

SEL Skills for Different School Levels	
Elementary School	social skills, positive attitude toward others, completion of tasks
Middle School	good self-esteem, reduced emotional distress, academic performance
High School	graduation, college readiness, healthy relationships, engaged citizenship

Some goals to support Kevin in managing himself in the classroom and in his interaction with his classmates would include focusing, listening attentively, dealing with conflict, and working cooperatively with his peers. One of the most prevalent SEL approaches involves training teachers to deliver explicit lessons that teach social and emotional skills, then finding opportunities for students to reinforce their use throughout the school day (Weissberg, 2016).

Interventions for Fostering SEL

A teacher can support students with social-emotional challenges to change their perspectives and behavior by relating to them in ways that foster acceptance in the classroom. Weissberg (2016) pointed out five strategies that can be beneficial for teachers supporting children in developing social-emotional skills.

1. Carry out supportive interactions.
   - Listen attentively by leaning forward, making eye contact, and asking questions.
   - A smile or thumbs-up can show you care while reassuring the student.
   - Letting students know you are happy to be their teacher by making small talk, sending notes home to acknowledge good behavior.
2. Foster supportive relationships between home and school.
   - Establish ways you can regularly communicate and/or exchange information with the students' caregiver.
   - Utilize family engagement events to ensure that families are involved with the child's education.
3. Provide activities and experiences that give children opportunities to learn social-emotional skills.
   - Help children build language and communication skills by asking open-ended questions throughout the day.
   - Encourage kindness and learn about feelings by reading books and singing songs about emotions.
   - Use mindfulness exercises that teach children appropriate ways to reduce stress and calm down.
4. Have a predictable yet flexible daily routine with carefully planned transitions.
   - Involve students in carrying out routines and transitions during the class day.
   - Teach students to take care of themselves by providing them with supplies for cleanup and personal care.

- Ensure that students do not feel rushed by planning enough time for activities and routines during the class day.
5. Design space to create learning environments that contribute to a child's overall development and well-being.
    - Create a space that makes children feel welcome and safe.
    - Encourage self-directed play and imagination.
    - Arrange the classroom space to allow children to be away from one another if needed.

Middle School

By the time students leave the primary grades to enter middle school, most understand why rules are necessary. Now, instead of behaving appropriately because of consequences, they follow rules and procedures because they can appreciate their reasonableness. Some students have a natural ability to attend to their emotions and some do not. For students with a limited ability to socially-emotionally regulate, it is important to build a rapport with these students and assist them in relearning new, effective ways to manage life tasks in and out of the classroom (Norris, 2003).

Vignette

Isabella, a twelve-year-old, has struggled with behavioral issues since she entered middle school. She comes late, attends class irregularly, is noncompliant toward her teachers, and complains that they are too strict and unfair when they insist that she abide by the same rules and do the same assignments as her classmates. Her parents are frustrated with Isabella's behavior but unsure how to handle the situation. During the few parent-teacher conferences they attended, they said they did not want to be too rigid with Isabella because it may cause her to act out even more at home. One of the teachers described them as being cooperative parents who did not enforce strict rules to avoid confrontations at home.

Teacher's Classroom Observation in *Addressing Social-Emotional Concerns*

Isabella is a student who has experienced social-emotional challenges prior to entering middle school. Isabella's behaviors, such as not following the school rules of attending class and completing assignments, may indicate a delayed development of age-appropriate social-emotional skills, self-management, relationship-building skills, and responsible decision-making. Indicators of delayed social-emotional regulation at this stage in development include ignoring teachers' directions, bullying other students, attending late or not attending class, expressing anger, and acting out in class.

Interventions for Fostering SEL

Teachers can help students with social-emotional challenges to acquire skills by creating a SEL environment that includes modeling appropriate behavior, explaining the practical necessity for rules and procedures, and helping students understand the effects of their behavior on others by providing students with cooperative learning experiences.

Some suggestions for establishing effective SEL environments include the following:

1. Creating a collaborative classroom
   - Having a classroom mission statement:
     What are the classroom expectations of the classroom climate?
     What will be the culture of the classroom?
   - Identifying what is required for students to feel safe, to feel accepted, and to be liked
   - Having regular morning meetings for students to check in and develop relationships with fellow students and teachers
2. Building respect within the classroom and among students
   - Openly acknowledging acts of kindness
   - Embedding opportunities for students to talk about feelings throughout the day
   - Developing sharing circles to promote inclusion and emphasize active listening and respect
3. Fostering cultural responsiveness
   - Incorporating a curriculum that addresses the value of accepting differences
   - Modeling acceptance rather than tolerance
   - Showing transparency by being interested in differences and celebrating those differences
4. Co-oping learning projects
   - Creating small group activities that allow students to relate to one another
   - Collaborating with community organizations that allow students to volunteer with diverse communities or populations

Teachers play an important role in socializing and emotionally nourishing students to develop their personal sense of competency and self-esteem. It is important to be proactive to create a student-friendly SEL environment.

Allocating informal time in and outside the class could give some students the personal attention they crave.

High School

Upon entering high school, most students have accepted the values of interacting and connecting with others, have internalized the social-emotional skills, and understand they need to control themselves in the absence of consequences. Students who lack social-emotional skills may have low self-esteem, poor academic performance, and emotional distress.

Vignette

> Ernie, a fifteen-year-old, was arrested for breaking into his school. He and two others removed audiovisual, musical, and office equipment worth several thousand dollars. Ernie had a history of stealing from other students when he was in elementary school, but that appeared to have stopped once he entered middle school, though one of his teachers suspected, but could not prove, that he continued to steal. In middle school and high school, he was suspected of copying homework, and he was observed cheating on tests a number of times, but he denied doing so when confronted by his teachers. His teachers considered him devious, dishonest, and manipulative but also bright enough to avoid being caught with the "smoking gun." When asked why he had broken into the school, Ernie claimed that he stole the equipment to get money to buy the clothes and other things he needed for school and a guitar to take guitar lessons because there were no jobs for someone his age and his mother wouldn't help him out.

Ernie lived with his mother and two sisters in a rundown neighborhood. His father was serving a second sentence for robbery. His mother advised the authorities to lock Ernie up with his father, since he had turned out to be "just like him."

Teacher's Classroom Observation in Addressing Social-Emotional Concerns

Ernie's behavior has had an impact in and outside of the classroom. Ernie appears to struggle with identity and social skills that promote social-emotional growth. Ernie has challenges with self-awareness, social awareness, relationship skills, and responsible decision-making. Ernie's family challenges the lack of structure at home as directly impacting his motivation for learning.

Ernie's challenges with identity and social-emotional skills at this stage in development are more likely to show the following behaviors in the classroom and school setting: destruction of school property, social isolation, disrespecting teachers and administrators, bullying other students, and school truancy.

Interventions for Fostering SEL

Teachers can support teenagers by working with them at their developmental stage to improve their social-emotional skills. The focus is to work with the "whole person" and meet the students where they are. Fostering SEL provides the foundation for a civil, safe, and positive learning environment that would enhance Ernie's ability to succeed. To effectively address Ernie's challenges within the classroom, it is important to help him feel he is an important part of the class (Weissberg, 2016).

Some interventions teachers can utilize in both the classroom and the school community to reinforce the development of social-emotional skills among high school students include the following:

1. Building a civil and respectful classroom environment
   - Acting in a caring and respectful manner toward students and openly acknowledging acts of goodwill
   - Providing opportunities for students to talk about their feelings throughout the day
   - Teaching social-emotional skills and giving students an opportunity to practice them in class and various situations
2. Fostering cultural responsiveness
   - Incorporating a curriculum that addresses the value of accepting differences in individuals
   - Modeling acceptance rather than tolerance
   - Being transparent by sharing your interests, being interested in differences, and celebrating differences among the students
3. Through SEL, addressing school culture
   - Identifying early signs of difficulty through prevention screening
   - Creating community partnerships that enhance resilience to social challenges (i.e., substance abuse prevention programs, college fairs, etc.)
   - Collaborating with community organizations that allow students to volunteer with diverse communities or populations
   - Creating school-family activities that encourage family members to engage with the school community

School and Community Roles in Fostering SEL

It is imperative to caution that allowing a child a voice is not the only pathway to prevention. Schools must cultivate and enforce a climate of civility. This can be achieved with a collaborative approach addressing classroom management, district and school policies, and family and community partnerships. Figure 7.1 highlights the connection between the community, the school district, and the classroom in fostering a SEL environment.

Classroom Management for *Promoting Positive Behavior*

Student inclusion in mainstream classrooms creates an environment where classroom management is paramount. Children may struggle at school because of learning challenges, social difficulties, and emotional or behavioral issues. The responsibility for their behavior in the learning environment can become the teacher's primary role due to the multitude of tasks that come with managing conduct and behavioral challenges in the classroom.

According to McMahon et al. (2006), these behaviors are correlated with stressed teacher-pupil relationships and poorer peer interaction in the classroom. To support conduct and behavioral challenges, district-wide and school-wide consistency is key to classroom management, as it fosters the adoption of behavioral norms in and out of the classroom setting (Nye et al., 2016).

At the school level, SEL strategies typically come in the form of policies, practices, or structures related to climate and student support services (Meyers et al., in press). Safe and positive school climates and cultures positively affect academic, behavioral, and mental health outcomes for students (Thapa et al., 2013). School leaders play a critical role in fostering school-wide activities and policies that promote positive school environments, such as establishing a team to address the building climate; modeling social and emotional competence; and developing clear norms, values, and expectations for students and staff members.

Fair and equitable discipline policies and bullying prevention practices are more effective than purely behavioral methods that rely on reward or punishment (Bear et al., 2015). School leaders can organize activities that build positive relationships and a sense of community among students through structures such as regularly scheduled morning meetings or advisories that provide students with opportunities to connect with one another (Weissberg, 2016).

An important component of school-wide SEL involves integration into multitiered systems of support. The services provided to students by professionals such as counselors, social workers, and psychologists should align

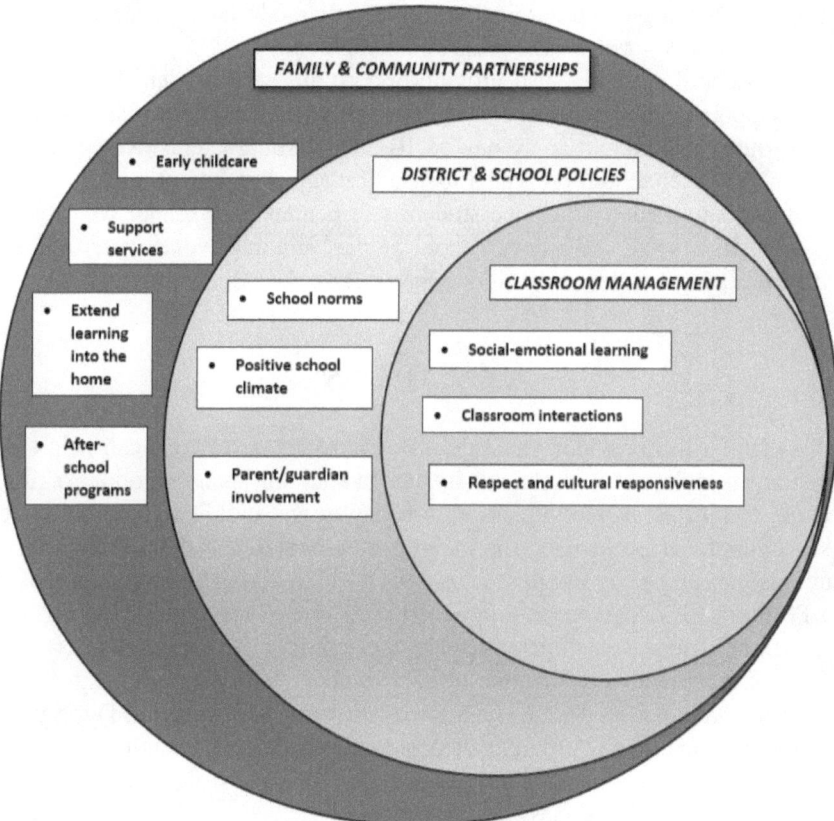

Figure 7.1 School and community collaboration for promoting SEL.

with universal school policies. Often through small-group work, student support professionals reinforce and supplement classroom-based instruction for students who need early intervention or more intensive treatment.

Building Family and Community Partnerships

SEL can also be fostered in many settings other than school. SEL begins in early childhood, so family and early childcare settings are important (Bierman & Motamedi, 2015). Higher education settings also have the potential to promote SEL (Conley, 2015).

Family and community partnerships can strengthen the impact of school approaches by extending learning into the home and neighborhood. Community members and organizations can support classroom and school efforts, especially by providing students with additional opportunities to refine and apply various SEL skills (Catalano et al., 2004).

After-school activities also provide opportunities for students to connect with supportive adults and peers (Gullotta, 2015). They are a great venue to help youth develop and apply new skills and personal talents. Research has shown that after-school programs focused on social and emotional development can significantly enhance student self-perceptions, school connectedness, positive social behaviors, school grades, and achievement test scores, while reducing problem behaviors (Durlak et al., 2011).

CONCLUSION

This chapter has provided techniques to address how teachers can help elementary, middle, and high school students in attaining social-emotional skills. While doing this, fostering classroom behavior and building community are paramount to support students in their development of social-emotional skills and maintaining a classroom structure for a rich learning environment.

Fostering SEL has become more difficult due to the current COVID-19 pandemic. Thus, it is imperative that the community, school district, and class management work together to help students who lack social-emotional skills navigate the challenges of a virtual learning environment. During the pandemic, teachers can promote classroom interactions and continue to foster respect to help students maintain a connection to the school and fellow classmates while in a virtual classroom setting.

As part of the transition to online learning and maintaining a connection to the overall school environment, school districts can work with parents and students by providing the necessary tools. This in turn allows students to have a continued sense of the school community by fostering extended learning in the home. Given the current changes within the education system as well as inclusive classrooms having physical, intellectual, and emotional needs to be addressed, teachers must discover new ways to meet the needs of all students utilizing universal methods identified in this chapter.

REFERENCES

Bandura, A. (1976). *Social learning theory*. Pearson Education.

Bear, G. G., Whitcomb, S. A., Elias, M. J., & Blank, J. C. (2015). SEL and schoolwide positive behavioral interventions and supports. In J. A. Durlak, C. E. Domitrovich, R. P. Weissberg, & T. P. Gullotta (Eds.), *Handbook of social and emotional learning* (pp. 458–67). Guilford Press.

Bierman, K. L., & Motamedi, M. (2015). SEL programs for preschool children. In J. A. Durlak, C. E. Domitrovich, R. P. Weissberg, & T. P. Gullotta (Eds.), *Handbook of social and emotional learning* (pp. 135–50). Guilford Press.

Blum, R. W., & Libbey, H. P. (2004). School connectedness: Strengthening the health and education outcomes for teenagers. *Journal of School Health, 74*(4), 229–99.

Bowlby, J. (1969). *Attachment and loss*. Basic Books.

Bridgeland, J., Bruce, M., & Hariharan, A. (2014). *The missing piece: A national survey on how social and emotional learning can empower children and transform schools*. Civic Enterprises.

Catalano, R. F., Berglund, M. L., Ryan, J. A., Lonczak, H. S., & Hawkins, J. D. (2004). Positive youth development in the United States: Research findings on evaluations of positive youth development programs. *Annals of the American Academy of Political and Social Science, 591*(1), 98–124.

Conley, C. S. (2015). SEL in higher education. In J. A. Durlak, C. E. Domitrovich, R. P. Weissberg, & T. P. Gullotta (Eds.), *Handbook of social and emotional learning* (pp. 197–212). Guilford Press.

Collaborative for Academic, Social, and Emotional Learning. (2020). *What is SEL?* Retrieved from https://casel.org/what-is-sel/.

Darling-Hammond, L., Flook, L., Cook-Harvey, C., Barron, B., & Osher, D. (2019). Implications for educational practice of the science of learning and development. *Applied Developmental Science, 24*(2), 97–140. 10.1080/10888691.2018.1537791.

Durlak, J. A., Weissberg, R. P., Dymnicki, A. B., Taylor, R. D., & Schellinger, K. B. (2011). The impact of enhancing students' social and emotional learning: A meta-analysis of school-based universal interventions. *Child Development, 82*(1), 405–43.

Green, F. E. (1999). Brain and learning research: Implications for meeting the needs of diverse learners. *Education-Indianapolis, 119*(1), 682–87.

Gullotta, T. P. (2015). After-school programming and SEL. In J. A. Durlak, C. E. Domitrovich, R. P. Weissberg, & T. P. Gullotta (Eds.), *Handbook of social and emotional learning* (pp. 260–81). Guilford Press.

Jennings, P. A., & Greenberg, M. T. (2009). The prosocial classroom: Teaching social and emotional competence in relations to child and classroom outcomes. *Review of Educational Research, 70*(1), 491–525.

Kaplan Early Learning. (2020). *Meeting the social-emotional needs of young children*. Retrieved from https://www.kaplanco.com/ii/meet-social-emotional-needs.

McMahon, R. J., Wells, K. C., & Kotler, J. S. (2006). Conduct problems in treatment of childhood disorders. In E. J. Mash & R. A. Barkley (Eds.), *Treatment of disorders in childhood and adolescence* (pp. 137–268). New York: Guilford Press.

Meyers, D., Gil, L., Cross, R., Keister, S., Domitrovich, C. E., & Weissberg, R. P. (in press). *CASEL guide for schoolwide social and emotional learning*. Collaborative for Academic, Social, and Emotional Learning.

National Alliance on Mental Illness. (2020). *Mental health in schools*. Retrieved from https://www.nami.org/Advocacy/Policy-Priorities/Intervene-Early/Mental-Health-in-Schools.

New York State Education Department. (2018). *Mental health education literacy in schools: Linking to a continuum of well-being.* Retrieved from http://www.nysed.gov/common/nysed/files/programs/curriculum-instruction/mental-health-education-one-pagerupdated9.24.2018-002.pdf.

Norris, J. A., (2003). Looking at classroom management through a social and emotional learning lens. *Theory into Practice, 42*(4), 313–18.

Nye, E., Gardner, F., Hansford, L., Edwards, V., Hayes, R., & Ford, T. (2016). Classroom behavior management strategies in response to problematic behaviours of primary school children with special education needs: Views of special educational needs coordinators. *Journal of Emotional and Behavioral Difficulties, 21*(1), 43–60.

Rivera, I. (2020). Cultural humility: My journey from personal experience to classroom teaching. *Reflections: Narratives of Professional Helping, 26*(2), 20–27.

Saphier, J. (2009). The equitable classroom: Today's diversity student body needs culturally proficient teachers. *Learning Professional, 38*(6), 28–31.

Schiering, M. (2017). *What's right with you: An interactive character development guide.* Rowman & Littlefield International.

Tatum, D. B. (1997). *Why are all the black kids sitting together in the cafeteria?* Basic Books.

Taylor, R. D., Oberle, E., Durlak, J. A., & Weissberg, R. P. (2017). Promoting positive youth development through school-based social and emotional learning interventions: A meta-analysis of follow-up effects. *Child Development, 88*(4), 1156–71.

Thapa, A., Cohen, J., Guffey, S., & Higgins-D'Alessandro, A. (2013). A review of school climate research. *Review of Educational Research, 83*(3), 357–85.

Weissberg, R. (2016). *Why social and emotional learning is essential for students: Learn more about the critical role that social and emotional learning plats in promoting student success.* Retrieved from https://www.edutopia.org/blog/why-sel-essential-for-students-weissberg-durlak-domitrovich-gullotta#:~:text=More%20positive%20attitudes%20toward%20oneself,problems%20and%20risk%2Dtaking%20behavior.

Zastrow, C. H., Kirst-Ashman, K. K., & Hessenauer, S. L. (2019). *Understanding human behavior in the social environment.* Cengage.

Index

AACTE. *See* American Association of Colleges for Teacher Education
academics: goals in, 95; K-12 teachers conveying expectations in, 111; student's readiness for, 98; teachers nourishing competency in, 131–32; trajectories in, 107
achievement goal model, 14–15
ADHD. *See* attention deficit hyperactivity disorder
Affective Networks, 63, 65–68
agents of change, 118–19
Ahmed, S. K., 35
Alcruz, J., 2
Alternative Teaching, 71
alternative teaching model, 74–75
American Association of Colleges for Teacher Education (AACTE), 48
American Revolution, 59–60
Americans with Disabilities Act (1990), 63
ASD. *See* autism spectrum disorder
Asia Society, 81
asset-based approach, 4–5
attainment value, 14
attention deficit hyperactivity disorder (ADHD), 56
attribution theory, 8

authoritarian approach, of classroom management, 11–12
authority figures, 40, 122
autism spectrum disorder (ASD), 56
autonomy support, 10

Backwards Design planning process, 58
Bandura, Albert, 98
Baumrind, D., 11
behaviors: adverse school, 115; caring, 125–26; classroom expectations of, 123–24; in classroom management, 2–3, 31, 94; college skills of, 112–13; communication strategies and, 94; maladaptive, 115–17, 134–35; positive, 134–35; prosocial, 120; social-emotional regulation of, 117–18, 128–29; student's maladaptive, 115–17; teacher's role in classroom, 119–20
Bernard, S. C., 81
Bible, King James, 80
Bible Riots, 80
Birkenstein-Graff, C., 96
Bishop, Rudine Sims, 36–37
Blair, M., 2
Blömeke, Sigrid, 3
brain development, 117–18
brain research, 56

Brewster, Edverette, 34
Brophy, J., 79
bullying, 134
Burkins, J., 97

caring behavior, 125–26
carrot and stick approach, 7
Center for Applied Special Technology (CAST), 63, 65–68
Cherng, H. S., 46
children: SEL development by, 129–30; social-emotional regulation of, 127–28; validation feeling for, 122
Churchill, Winston S., 7
classroom community: strategies building, 36–37; for student learning, 34–39, 106; student voices in, 43
Classroom Dojo (tool), 8
classroom management: communications used for, 94–99; complex factors in, 75; co-teaching in, 69–70; culturally responsive, 31; disruptions reduced through, 101; enhanced approaches to, 3; motivation used in, 10–11; positive behavior promoted for, 134–35; practices and procedures in, 30; proactive communication strategies for, 5; student behaviors in, 2–3, 31, 92; student-centered learning environment in, 75–76
classrooms: behavioral expectations for, 123–24; collaborative, 131; cultures and diversity in, 79–80, 86–89; equitable procedures in, 41; families receiving information from, 37; mission statements for, 124; motivational strategies in, 21, *22*; personalized learning in, 4; Restorative Circles addressing issues in, 42; restorative practices implementation in, 41–44; restorative practices in, 39–40; social-emotional concerns in, 126–36; social-emotional skills in, 127; structures in, 15–16; student learning strategies in, 4; teacher's role in behaviors in, 121–22
Coates, Ta-Nehesi, 47
cognition, 16–17, 98
collaborative classrooms, 131
college: behavioral skills for, 112–13; higher-level learning and, 96–98; middle school readiness for, 97; self-accountability in, 110
communication partnerships, 106–8
communications: classroom management using, 94–99; for grade-level transitions, 108–12; proactive strategies in, 5; student flexibility through, 111–12; teacher's skills in, 93–94; transformative experiences from, 109–10
communication strategies, 93; for classroom management, 5; content rationale explained in, 103–4; dialogue engagement in, 100–102; for grade-level transitions, 95–98, 112; inquiry-based learning fostered by, 104–6; objectives achieved through, 94–95; positives accentuated in, 99, 102–103; structure of, 109; student's behavior and, 94; for teachers, 112
community, 118, 135–36
compassion, 123, 124, 125
competitive structures, 15
compromise, failure to, 60
Connect the Dots (Taylor, T., and Dibner), 18
"Conscious Responsive Classrooms" conference, 1
constructive feedback, 13
content rationale, 103–4
Cook, L., 70
cooperative learning, 125
cooperative structures, 15
corporal punishment, 80
Costello, B., 39, 43
cost value, 14

co-teaching: alternative teaching model in, 74–75; in classroom management, 69–70; models, 69–75; one teach, one observe model in, 72–74; for personalized learning, 72; for UDL, 73
COVID-19, 31, 136
critical thinking, 17, 104–5
Culturally Responsive-Sustaining Education Framework, 2, 33, 49, 86, 89
cultures: classroom diversity and, 86–89; classroom management responsive to, 31; defining, 48; diverse students and, 116; in education, 85; education's historical perspectives of, 79–82; teachers responsive to, 126, 131, 133; teachers understanding students, 48–49. *See also* ethnicity; race
Cyclical Phases Model, of SRL, 16

The Day You Begin (Woodson), 32

de Brey, C., 82
Deci, E. L., 9, 21, 98
decision making, 61, 127
deep listening, 101
demographics, U.S. changing, 89
Department of Education, 84
Dewey, John, 55
dialogue, 99–102
Dibner, N., 18
differentiated instruction, 66–67, 74
disruptions, classroom, 101
diversity, 2; classrooms with culture and, 79–80, 86–89; of elementary students, 33; empathy with perspectives of, 124; personalized learning for, 4; in public schools, 81–82; in schools, 116; teacher preparation including, 50
dual coding, 18
Dweck, Carol, 13, 36

easy lift, 99, 100
edTPA, 48
education: cultures in, 85; higher, 4, 48–49; historical-cultural perspectives of, 79–82; social-emotional skills of, 127; special, 71
Education for All Handicapped Children Act, 55, 82
Egalite, A. J., 46
elaboration, 18
Elementary and Secondary Education Act (ESEA), 82
elementary-grade students, 33, 104–5
elementary schools: brain development during, 117; social-emotional skills in, 127–28; teachers, 4
ELLs. *See* English-Language Learners
emotional response, 105
empathy: behavioral expectations for, 123–24; caring behavior for, 125–26; compassion and, 120, 124, 125; cooperative learning for, 125; diverse perspectives for, 124; perspective taking for, 123; social awareness for, 125; teachers incorporating, 123–26
empowerment, 3, 45
engagement, by students, 3, 32–34, 97
Engagement Networks, 68
English-Language Learners (ELLs), 83–85
equitable procedures, 41
equity, 2
ESEA. *See* Elementary and Secondary Education Act
ESOL learning, 55
ESSA. *See* Every Student Succeeds Act
ethnicity: of elementary students, 33; student and teacher as same, 46; in U.S., 83. *See also* cultures; race
ethnocentrism, 80
Every Student Succeeds Act (ESSA), 82
expectancy-value theory, 8
expectations: classroom behavior, 123–24; motivational theories related to, 12; in student learning, 12–14;

of teachers, 19–20, 82–83; teachers K-12 conveying, 111
explicit instructions, 18
extrinsic motivation, 9–10
extrinsic value, 14

families: classroom information shared with, 37; journal entry of, 38–39; SEL community partnerships with, 135–36; teacher's partnerships with, 37–39. *See also* children
feedback, 8, 13, 19
Finley, T., 85
Fishbowl Circles, 42–43, *43*
Fletcher, Ralph, 32
Free Appropriate Public Education, 63
Friend, Marilyn, 70–72, 74

Gay, G., 47
Ginott, H., 34
goal setting, 61
grade-level transitions: communications for, 108–12; communication strategies for, 95–98, 112; learning environment and, 110; personalized learning for, 100
Graff, G., 96
Graham, E. J., 44
Great Depression, 81
Great Wave of Immigration, 81
Growth Mindset theory (Dweck), 13

Halpin, P. F., 46
Harvard Teaching Fellow program, 34, 46

The Hate U Give (Thomas), 32

Haycock, K., 47
heavy lift, 99, 100
Herold, Benjamin, 55
higher education, 4, 48–49
higher-level learning, 96–98
high school students, 133

historical-cultural perspectives, of education, 79–82
Huerta, G., 80
human relationships, 40

identity, challenges of, 132–33
IEPs. *See* Individual Education Plans
immigration: Irish Catholic, 81; population shift from, 82; to U.S., 80
inclusive learning environment, 124
Individual Education Plans (IEPs), 56, 65–66, 128
individual guidance, 104
individualistic structures, 16
individual lessons, 65–66
Individuals with Disabilities Acts, 82
Individuals with Disabilities Education Act, 55, 65, 71
inquiry-based learning, 104–6
Interactions (Friend and Cook), 70
interleaving, 18
internalization, 11
intrinsic motivation, 9–10, 20–21
intrinsic value, 14
Irish Catholic immigrants, 81

Jacobson, L., 20
Jefferson, Thomas, 79–80
journal entry, 38–39

Kohn, Alfie, 2, 10
Kozol, Jonathan, 34

Ladson-Billings, Gloria, 86
language, 35–36
Lau v. Nichols, 82
Learning Cycles, 66–67
learning environment: cooperation in, 125; grade-level transitions and, 110; inclusive, 124; inquiry-based, 104–6; SEL fostered in, 118, 131–32; student-centered, 75–76; teachers creating positive, 86–88, 98. *See also* student learning

learning experience, teacher-centered, 61

The Learning Scientists, 17

learning strategies, research-supported, 17–18
Leibel, Sarah, 48
Leitão, N., 85
Letters to a Young Teacher (Kozol), 34
linkages, 103–4
listening: deep, 101; power of, 122; teacher's role of, 101–102

maladaptive behaviors, 115–17, 134–35
Mann, Horace, 80
Marzano, J. S., 47
Marzano, R. J., 30, 32, 47, 88
McGuffey, William H., 81
McMahon, R. J., 134
McTighe, Jay, 57–58, 61, 71
mental disorders, 115
meta-cognition, 18
middle school, 97, 130
mind-body connection, 118
mindfulness, 21
Mindset (Dweck), 36
mindset, of teachers, 35–36, 56
mission statements, for classrooms, 124
mixed-ability groups, 74–75
MLLs. *See* multilingual learners
modeling, 18
Molloy College Lesson Plan, 4
Mondale, S., 81
motivation: classroom management using, 10–11; classroom strategies using, 21, *22*; definitions of, 8–10; expectancies related to theories of, 12; extrinsic and intrinsic, 9–10, 20–21; self-efficacy beliefs for, 9; SRL connected to, 19; student learning approaches using, 7
multilingual learners (MLLs), 83–85
multitiered support systems, 134–35

National Universal Design for Learning Taskforce, 64
New York State Education Department, 86
No Child Left Behind, 82
nonsequential circle, 44
novice teachers, 3

One Teach, One Assist, 70
One Teach, One Observe, 70, 72–74

Parallel Teaching, 70–71
peer interactions, 134
permissive approach, of classroom management, 11
personalization, 94–95
personalized learning, 55–56; in classrooms, 4; co-teaching for, 72; for grade-level transitions, 100; individual lessons for, 65–66; UDL guidelines for, 65
perspective taking, 123
planning tool, for UDL, 64
Plessy v. Ferguson, 80
population shift, 82–85
Positive Behavior Interventions and Supports (tool), 8
positive behaviors, 134–35
positive feedback, 8
positive mindset, 49
positives, accentuating, 99, 102–103
proactive circle, 45–46
proactive communication strategies, 5
problem solving, 17
progress feedback, 19
prosocial behaviors, 120
psychology, dialogue in, 101
public schools, 80; diversity in, 81–82; population shifting in, 82–85
punishment, 41, 80
Pygmalion effect (self-fulfilling prophesy), 35
"Pygmalion in the Classroom" (Rosenthal and Jacobson), 20

race, 20, 46, *83*
Recognition Networks, 63, 66–67
reflection, 21
relationships: building, 11–12; collaborative, 107; human, 42; student achievement from, 34, 49–50; for student learning, 3–4, 32
Restorative Circles: benefits, 41–42; classroom issues addressed in, 42; Fishbowl Circles as, 42–43, *43*; types of, 45
restorative practices, 39–45
retrieval practice, 18
reward/punishment system, 8, 121
Roberts v. City of Boston, 80
Roll of Thunder, Hear My Cry (Taylor, M.), 47
Rosenthal, R., 20
Ryan, R. M., 9, 21, 98

safe environment, 86–88, 98, 125
same-ability groups, 74
SCALE. *See* Stanford Center for Assessment, Learning and Equity
school districts, 107
schools: adverse behaviors in, 115; as agents of change, 118–19; culturally diverse students in, 116; elementary, 4, 117, 127–28; high school students in, 133; middle, 97, 130; public, 80–85; SEL community partnerships with, 135, 135–36; SEL fostered in, 118–21; social-emotional skills in, 128. *See also* academics; college; education; learning environment
SEL. *See* Social-Emotional Learning
self-accountability, in college, 110
Self-Determination Theory, 9–11, 21
self-efficacy, 98; for motivation, 9; student habits of, 113; at task-specific level, 13; of teachers, 10
self-esteem, 85, 126, 131
self-fulfilling prophesy (Pygmalion effect), 35
self-management, 110

self-reflection, *87–88*
Self-Regulation of Learning (SRL), *17*; Cyclical Phases Model of, 16; meta-cognition in, 18; motivation connected to, 19; for students, 16
self-talk, 18
sequential circle, 43–44
Skinner, B. F., 8
Smith, D., 39
social awareness, 125
social cognitive theory, 8–9
social discipline, 40
Social-Emotional Learning (SEL), 5; children's development of, 129–30; COVID-19 influencing, 136; learning environment for, 118, 131–32; multitiered support systems for, 134–35; prosocial behaviors from, 120; school and community partnerships for, 135–36; schools fostering, 118–21; student learning from, 119; teachers programming, 120
social-emotional regulation: behavioral indicators for, 117–18, 128–29; of children, 127–28; classrooms with concerns for, 126–36; education with skills of, 127; elementary schools skills of, 127–28; of high school students, 133; in middle school, 130; schools with skills of, 128; of students, 5, 116–17, 132; from teachers, 120–21, 128–30; teachers addressing concerns of, 130–33
social learning theory, 122–23
soft skills, 97
solutions-based responses, 102
spaced practice, 17, 36
special education, 71
SRL. *See* Self-Regulation of Learning
Stahnke, Rebekka, 3
standardization, 94–95
Stanford Center for Assessment, Learning and Equity (SCALE), 48
Station Teaching, 70
stereotype threats, 13–14

Strategic Networks, 63, 66–68
Student-Centered Classrooms (Alcruz and Blair), 2
student-centered learning environment, 75–76
student learning: asset-based approach for, 4–5; classroom community for, 34–39, 106; classroom strategies for, 4; concepts understood for, 57–58; engaged attitude for, 97; ESOL, 55; expectancies in, 12–14; experiences in, 59; experiences planned for, 61–62; inquiry-based, 104–6; motivational approaches to, 7; positive mindset for, 49; race and, 20; relationships for, 3–4, 32; safe positive environment for, 86–88, 98, 125; SEL foundation for, 119; stereotype threats influencing, 13–14; teachers facilitating, 2; values related to, 14–16
students: academic readiness of, 98; active participation by, 101; agency of, 10; authority figures and, 40; books shared with, 37; classroom behavior of, 2–3, 31, 94; classroom community with voices of, 43; in communication partnerships, 106–8; communications for flexibility of, 111–12; cooperative learning for, 125; differentiated instruction for, 66–67; with effective teachers, 47; elementary-grade, 33, 104–5; engagement by, 3, 32–34, 97; hardships overcome by, 111; high school, 133; K–12, 110–11; labeling, 82; maladaptive behaviors of, 115–17; peer interactions of, 134; relationships for achievement of, 34, 49–50; with same-ethnicity teacher, 46; with same-race teacher, 46; school's with culturally diverse, 116; self-efficacy habits of, 113; social-emotional development of, 5; social-emotional regulation of, 5, 116–17, 132; SRL for, 16; teachers and cultural background of, 48–49; teacher's belief in capabilities of, 36; teacher's collaborative relationship with, 107; teachers culturally responsive to, 126, 131, 133; teacher's expectations of, 19–20, 82–83; teachers identifying struggling, 5, 93; teacher's interactions with, 11–12; teacher's role in achievement of, 29–30; teachers sensing emotional response of, 105; teachers understanding, 57; UbD centered around, 60–62; UDL approach to instructional goals of, 64

talking piece, 43
Taylor, Mildred, 47
Taylor, T., 18
teacher-centered learning experience, 61
teachers: academic competency nourished by, 131–32; authoritarian approach of, 11–12; authority figures influence of, 122; classroom behavior role of, 121–22; in communication partnerships, 106–8; communication skills of, 93–94; communication strategies of, 112; cooperative learning from, 125; co-teaching models for, 69–75; culturally responsive, 126, 131, 133; diversity preparation for, 50; elementary school, 4; empathy incorporated by, 123–26; expectations of, 19–20, 82–83; family partnerships with, 37–39; individual guidance from, 104; K–12 students guidance from, 110–11; learning facilitated by, 2; listening role of, 101–102; mindset and beliefs of, 35–36, 56; novice, 3; permissive approach of, 11; positive learning environment from, 86–88, 98; positives accentuated by, 99, 102–103; preparation courses for,

48; safe environment encouraged by, 86–88, 98, 123; with same-ethnicity students, 46; with same-race students, 46; self-efficacy of, 10; SEL programming from, 120; social-emotional concerns addressed by, 130–33; social-emotional regulation from, 120–21, 128–30; solutions-based responses by, 102; student achievement role of, 29–30; student's capabilities belief of, 36; student's collaborative relationship with, 107; student's cultural background and, 48–49; student's emotional response and, 105; student's interactions with, 11–12; student's relationships with, 3–4, 32; student struggles identified by, 5, 93; students with effective, 47; student understanding of, 57; UDL suggestions for, 65–68; understanding-based unit plan for, 59–61. *See also* co-teaching
teachers K-12: academic expectations conveyed by, 111; content understanding assured by, 104; higher-level learning preparations by, 96–98
Team Teaching, 71
Thomas, Angela, 32
Thousand, J. S., 69
Tomlinson, Carol Ann, 66, 71
transformative experiences, 109–10
Triangle of Responsibility, 69

UbD. *See* Understanding by Design
UDL. *See* Universal Design for Learning

understanding-based unit plan, 59–61
Understanding by Design (UbD): Backwards Design of, 58; principles of, 57–59; as student centered, 60–62
Understanding by Design Framework Guide (McTighe and Wiggins), 57, 61
United States (U.S.): adverse behaviors in schools of, 115; demographics changing in, 89; ELLs and MLLs in, 83–85; immigration to, 80; race and ethnicity in, 83
Universal Design for Learning (UDL), 62–63, 116; CAST's guidelines for, 65; co-teaching models for, 73; planning tool for, 64; student's instructional goals in, 64; suggestions for teachers from, 65–68
U.S. *See* United States

validation, of children, 122
values, students learning, 14–16
verbalization, 18

Walch, T., 81
Waugh, R., 85
Weissberg, R., 129
"Welcome to Co-Teaching 2.0" (Friend), 71, 74
Wiggins, Grant, 57–58, 61, 71
Winzer, M. A., 81–82
Wong, H. K., 30
Woodson, Jacqueline, 32
Workman, E., 35
Wright, S. P., 30

Zastrow, C. H., 127

About the Contributors

Joanna Alcruz, PhD, is an associate professor in the School of Education and Human Services at Molloy University and teaches in the Educational Leadership Doctoral Program for Diverse Communities. Her educational background includes educational psychology from Fordham University and measurement and evaluation from New York University. Dr. Alcruz's expertise is in cognition and learning, quantitative research, assessment, and research methods. Prior to becoming a faculty member, she served as an accreditation coordinator for the School of Education at Molloy University. Her research focus is on self-regulated learning, motivation, academic procrastination, and divergent thinking. She has presented her studies at local and national educational conferences and teacher professional development sessions, offered workshops and webinars on how to navigate learning, and written several professional publications. She is a cofounder and codirector of the Cognition and Learning Lab at Molloy University.

Maggie Blair, MA, received her degree in special education from New York University and a professional diploma in district administration. She has spent almost fifty years in the field of special education, serving as a teacher, a staff developer, and an administrator in New York City, and then as the district administrator in several school districts on Long Island. During her tenure in school districts, Maggie developed and initiated successful co-teaching models that supported classified students as they returned to general education settings. Her models were replicated by several districts. She joined the faculty at Molloy University of a newly established Master's Program in Special Education in 2003 and served there until 2020. Prior to her retirement and following her lifelong goal to ensure that all students have the opportunity to access rich educational experiences, Maggie and a small group of passionate colleagues successfully designed, developed, and initiated an academic-based, employment-bound, and fully immersive college experience transition program, the MOST Program (Molloy Opportunity for Successful Transition), on the campus of Molloy University in September 2019.

Eve Dieringer, EdD, is a director of field placement at Molloy University's School of Education and Human Services. She also teaches an undergraduate course that focuses on the "Critical Issues in Education." Prior to her work at Molloy, Eve served as a reading specialist and then as an administrator in public education on Long Island, New York. Literacy remains her passion. She has written several articles regarding student teaching and has presented for state-level professional organizations.

Michael J. Ferretti is the district director of strategic planning and safety in Copiague School District. Prior to that, he was assistant principal at Copiague Middle School and served as chairperson of the English Department at the Walter G. O'Connell Copiague High School. Mr. Ferretti is presently an adjunct professor at Molloy University in the School of Education and Human Services. He is interested in professional development and has been a keynote speaker to preservice and in-service teachers at Molloy University. He received the Educator of Excellence Award from the New York State English Council in 2013.

Amandia Speakes-Lewis, PhD, LCSW-R, is an associate professor of social work in the School of Education and Human Services at Molloy University in Rockville Centre, New York. She is an educator and clinician with over 25 years of experience. Dr. Speakes-Lewis is a New York State Licensed Clinical Social Worker with a master's degree and PhD in social work from Stony Brook University and Adelphi University. Her knowledge base, writing, and research are in the areas of behavioral health, stress management, and microaggressions.

Carrie McDermott Goldman, EdD, is associate professor and coordinator of Graduate and Post-Graduate TESOL/Bilingual Programs at Molloy University, Rockville Centre, New York. Carrie is passionate about working with preservice and in-service teachers and administrators to focus on equitable educational practices for multicultural learners, and recently, she has coauthored the book *From Equity Insights to Action: Critical Strategies for Teaching Multilingual Learners*. Prior to higher education, she taught pre-K–12 in high needs settings and college-level ESL. To meet the growing needs of multilingual learners throughout the region, she coauthored several book chapters, including *Co-Taught Integrated Language and Mathematics Content Instruction for Multilingual Learners*; *Positive Outcomes for ELs in an Integrated Social Studies Class*; *Preparing Social Studies and ESOL*

Teachers for Integrated Language and Content Instruction; and *Preparing Science Teachers for Project-based, Integrated, Collaborative Instruction.* In addition, she serves as the director and principal investigator of the New York State Grant for the U.S. Department of Education, *Clinically Rich Intensive Teachers Institute in Bilingual Education and TESOL (CR-ITI BE/ESOL)*. She continues to collaborate with schools as an instructional coach, curriculum developer, and mentor for teachers and administrators.

Amy Meyers, PhD, LCSW, is an associate professor of social work and director of field education at Molloy University in Rockville Centre, New York. Dr. Meyers is an expert on sibling abuse and has published and presented nationally on the topic. She also has a strong interest in social justice and has focused on bullying, publishing on the topic of building a culture of acceptance. Her interest in diversity and inclusion propelled her to collaborate on the development of an office of Social Justice at her college. In partnership, Dr. Meyers has developed an Interfaith/Interracial Dialogue program to address education inequity on the Molloy campus and in the community and is currently transforming a local school district's approach to culturally competent and inclusive teaching. As a professor, researcher, therapist, and friend, she has addressed classroom and behavioral management for several decades. She maintains a culturally diverse private practice in New York City.

Youn-Joo Park, PhD, is an assistant professor of communications at State University of New York–Farmingdale, where she teaches undergraduate courses in culture and communications, digital journalism, media literacy, and technical communications. In addition, she provides editorial consulting for Molloy University and Brushcase Editing. Her professional experiences are in broadcast media, print/digital journalism, and publishing. Over the past two decades, she has also worked as an academic tutor and piano teacher to K–12 students.

Lisa Peluso, EdD, is an assistant professor of childhood education at Molloy University in Rockville Centre, New York. She taught elementary school for thirteen years in New York City and prior to this was an English as a Second Language instructor at Queens College, City University of New York. She is the author of *Religious Sister Educators: A Narrative Study through a Feminist Lens* (2019), coauthor of *Pre-Service ESL Teachers' Instructional Discourse* (2009), and a contributor to *Core Instructional Routines: Go to Structures for Effective Literacy Teaching K-5* (2014). She has presented at various educational conferences and teacher professional development sessions, exploring topics ranging from interpreting and utilizing standardized testing data for more effective instruction to her most recent work on infusing social-emotional learning practices with social justice leadership principles to promote greater equity in classrooms and schools.

Mubina Schroeder, PhD, is an associate professor in the School of Education and Human Services at Molloy University. Dr. Schroeder teaches graduate- and doctoral-level courses in cognitive sciences, science pedagogy, and neurodiversity. She has her educational training in neuroscience, cognition, and science pedagogy and has worked on research projects with Dr. Carol Dweck's Brainology initiative, the U.S. Department of Energy, New York University, and the Federal Reserve Bank of New York. She is the recipient of the *New York Times Teachers Who Make a Difference Award* for her work as a New York City public school science teacher, and she was twice granted the Einstein Distinguished Educator Fellowship by the U.S. Department of Energy to research increasing engagement in science classrooms. Dr. Schroeder was elected to the Executive Board of Directors at the Global NGO Committee at the United Nations, where her projects focused on initiatives to increase awareness of climate change issues in classrooms by utilizing personal experiences. She currently serves as a codirector of the Cognition and Learning Lab at Molloy University.

Kevin Sheehan, EdD, is a retired associate professor from Molloy University who has currently transitioned into teaching in a pioneer Molloy Opportunities for Successful Transitions program for young adults with special needs. During his fifteen-year tenure at Molloy University, Dr. Sheehan was honored with the Distinguished Service Medal (2019) and the Molloy Faculty Leadership Award (2013). Prior to joining Molloy, Dr. Sheehan enjoyed an extensive career as a social studies educator and administrator in the Oceanside School System. He received recognition as the Distinguished Social Studies Educator in New York State (2009–2010), the Presidential Leadership Award from the Long Island Council for Social Studies, and the New York State Social Studies Supervisor of the Year (2006). Dr. Sheehan is most recently known for his research, presentations, and journal articles on hope and grit in the field of positive psychology, authoring numerous publications, among them two well-received books, *Growing a Growth Mindset: Unlocking Character Strengths through Children's Literature* and *Winning the Game of Belief: Cultivating the Cultural Grit That Defines America's Greatest Coaches*.

Carrie Sollin, EdD, is a licensed mental health counselor and an associate director at Triangle Cognitive Therapy, PPC, in Rockville Centre, New York. She also teaches undergraduate psychology courses as an adjunct assistant professor at Adelphi University, Garden City, New York. Dr. Sollin has recently earned her doctorate from the Educational Leadership for Diverse Learning Communities EdD program at Molloy University in Rockville Centre, New York, with her research focus on gatekeeper suicide prevention training for faculty in higher education. She is passionate about merging the fields of education and mental health and feels teaching students holistically will bring students to their highest potentials, personally and academically. Dr. Sollin has been in the field of education and psychology for twenty years and has presented at several conferences. Most recently, she presented at the Higher Education Suicide Prevention Conference (HESPC) at Penn State in May 2018 on the importance of training faculty to identify, approach, and refer students with all their mental health needs.

Kathleen Neagle Sokolowski is an educator with nineteen years of teaching experience in the elementary grades. Neagle Sokolowski has certification in elementary education, special education, and literacy studies. She is the codirector of the Long Island Writing Project and a coauthor for the popular blog *Two Writing Teachers*. In 2016, she was awarded the New York State English Council Educator of Excellence Award (Elementary). Neagle Sokolowski's heart is in helping children grow in their literacy skills and believing in themselves as learners.